JOSEPH

CHARACTERS OF THE BIBLE SERIES
BY JIMMY SWAGGART:

Jacob

Great Women of the Bible, New Testament

Great Women of the Bible, Old Testament

Abraham

Noah

David

Paul

JOSEPH

JIMMY SWAGGART

Jimmy Swaggart Ministries
P.O. Box 262550 | Baton Rouge, Louisiana 70826-2550
Website: www.jsm.org | Email: info@jsm.org | Phone: 225.768.7000

ISBN 978-1-941403-04-4

09-124 | COPYRIGHT © 2014 Jimmy Swaggart Ministries®

14 15 16 17 18 19 20 21 22 23 / RRD / 10 9 8 7 6 5 4 3 2 1

JOSEPH TABLE OF CONTENTS

JOSEPH

INTRODUCTION

INTRODUCTION

I BELIEVE THAT one can say without fear of contradiction that there is no story, no illustration, and no experience in history that even remotely equals that of Joseph, the son of Jacob. He was sold as a slave into Egypt by his wicked brothers, which was a fate worse than death. His father was made to believe that Joseph had been killed by wild beasts. He was then placed in prison because of being falsely accused. After that, he was made the governor of all of Egypt, the second most powerful man in the world of that time. Only God could do such a thing.

How long Joseph remained in prison before becoming governor, the Scripture does not say. We know that it was longer than two years, and possibly as many as seven. At any rate, the Scripture says of this time, *"He (the Lord) sent a man before them, even Joseph, who was sold for a servant:*

"Whose feet they hurt with fetters: he was laid in iron:

"Until the time that His Word came: the Word of the Lord tried him" (Ps. 105:17-19).

THE QUESTION

Joseph was a type of Christ, consequently, he is the only man in the Bible where no sin is recorded against him. Of course, we know that he did sin because the Scripture plainly tells us that *"all have sinned, and come short of the glory of God"* (Rom. 3:23).

It would have been a simple thing for the Lord to have delivered him from prison, meaning that he not go there in the first place, but is it possible that the Lord allowed this situation for Joseph's sake? How long could he have stood up under the onslaught of the temptation that was presented to him? The Spirit is willing but the flesh is weak.

I am not saying that this was the cause of his imprisonment, but I am saying that the possibility definitely does exist.

Joseph's life was one of prophetic circumstance regarding his people Israel, who had not yet come into being.

THE WORD OF THE LORD

What I'm about to give is that which I believe the Lord gave me concerning Pharaoh and the dream given to that monarch some 3,700 years ago, and most important of all, the interpretation given by Joseph.

The dream given to the monarch — a heathen, we might quickly add, who did not know the Lord — came in two parts, which I will quote verbatim from *The Expositor's Study Bible*:

"And it came to pass at the end of two full years, that Pharaoh dreamed: and, behold, he stood by the river (*as to exactly how long that Joseph spent in prison, we aren't told; however, we do know that he stayed there two more years after the interpretation of the dream given to the chief butler*).

"And, behold, there came up out of the river seven well favored cattle and fatfleshed; and they fed in a meadow.

"And, behold, seven other cattle came up after them out of the river, ill favored and leanfleshed; and stood by the other cattle upon the brink of the river.

"And the ill favored and leanfleshed cattle did eat up the seven well favored and fat cattle. So Pharaoh awoke.

"And he slept and dreamed the second time: and, behold, seven ears of corn (*either barley or wheat, for there was no corn in that part of the world at that time, as we know of such presently*) came up upon one stalk, rank and good.

"And, behold, seven thin ears and blasted with the east wind sprung up after them.

"And the seven thin ears devoured the seven rank and full ears. And Pharaoh awoke, and, behold, it was a dream.

INTERPRETATION SOUGHT

"And it came to pass in the morning that his spirit was troubled; and he sent and called for all the magicians of Egypt, and all the wise men thereof: and Pharaoh told them his dream; but there was none who could interpret them unto Pharaoh. (The Egyptian Book of the Dead, *now in the British Museum in London, with its sacred cows and mystic number seven — a book beyond doubt well known to Pharaoh — must have helped to convince the king that this double dream was supernatural.)*

"Then spoke the chief butler unto Pharaoh, saying, I do remember my faults this day *(with none of the magicians able to interpret the dream, or at least to Pharaoh's satisfaction, it began to be known in the palace as to the dilemma, until it reached the chief butler):*

"Pharaoh was angry with his servants, and put me in ward in the captain of the guard's house, both me and the chief baker:

"And we dreamed a dream in one night, I and he; we dreamed each man according to the interpretation of his dream.

"And there was there with us a young man, an Hebrew, servant to the captain of the guard; and we told him, and he interpreted to us our dreams; to each man according to his dream he did interpret.

"And it came to pass, as he interpreted to us, so it was; me he *(you)* restored unto mine office, and him he *(you)* hanged.

THE INTERPRETATION GIVEN

"Then Pharaoh sent and called Joseph, and they brought him hastily out of the dungeon: and he shaved himself, and changed his raiment, and came in unto Pharaoh. *(Events now transpire which no human hand could manipulate. Only God could do such a thing. This should teach us that we should allow the Lord to plan for us. Men forgot Joseph, but it is double certain that God didn't forget Joseph. And neither will He forget you. This is at least one of the reasons that we must look to God instead of men.)*

"And Pharaoh said unto Joseph, I have dreamed a dream, and there is none who can interpret it: and I have heard say of you, that you can understand a dream to interpret it. *(The Lord, once again, uses dreams to reveal His will.)*

"And Joseph answered Pharaoh, saying, It is not in me: God shall give Pharaoh an answer of peace. *(Joseph could have claimed great things, but instead he gave all the glory to God for giving him the interpretation of these dreams.)*

"And Pharaoh said unto Joseph, In my dream, behold, I stood upon the bank of the river *(the Nile River)*:

"And, behold, there came up out of the river seven cattle, fatfleshed and well favored; and they fed in a meadow:

"And, behold, seven other cattle came up after them, poor and very ill favored and leanfleshed, such as I never saw in all the land of Egypt for badness:

"And the lean and the ill favored cattle did eat up the first seven fat cattle:

"And when they had eaten them up, it could not be known that they had eaten them; but they were still ill favored, as at the beginning. So I awoke.

THE SEVEN EARS OF GRAIN

"And I saw in my dream, and, behold, seven ears came up in one stalk, full and good:

"And, behold, seven ears, withered, thin, and blasted with the east wind, sprung up after them:

"And the thin ears devoured the seven good ears: and I told this unto the magicians; but there was none that could declare it to me.

"And Joseph said unto Pharaoh, The dream of Pharaoh is one: God has showed Pharaoh what He is about to do. (*The dream was doubled, in order, as Joseph says in Verse 32, to denote its divine certainty and, as well, to portray its immediate happening, as well as its futuristic happening.*)

SEVEN YEARS OF PLENTY

"The seven good cattle are seven years; and the seven good ears are seven years: the dream is one.

"And the seven thin and ill favored cattle that came up after them are seven years; and the seven empty ears blasted with the east wind shall be seven years of famine. (*Discoveries many years ago at the First Cataract, and at El-Kab, record the fact of this seven years famine. The date is given as 1700 B.C. This date accords with accepted Bible chronology.*)

"This is the thing which I have spoken unto Pharaoh: What God is about to do He shows unto Pharaoh.

"Behold, there come seven years of great plenty throughout all the land of Egypt:

"And there shall arise after them seven years of famine; and all the plenty shall be forgotten in the land of Egypt; and the famine shall consume the land;

"And the plenty shall not be known in the land by reason of that famine following; for it shall be very grievous.

"And for that the dream was doubled unto Pharaoh twice; it is because the thing is established by God, and God will shortly bring it to pass" (Gen. 41:1-32).

ONE DREAM, TWO PARTS

As is obvious, Pharaoh had one dream but in two parts.

The seven fat cattle represented seven years of the greatest food harvest that Egypt had ever known. The seven lean cattle represented seven years of famine that would come upon Egypt and the Middle East. It took that seven years of famine to bring Jacob to Joseph.

I believe that the second part of the dream has not yet been fulfilled.

I personally believe that the seven withered ears of grain represent the coming great tribulation that Daniel said would last seven years. It will be the worst time in the history of the world (Mat. 24:21). It will take that to bring Jacob to Jesus, as it took that so long ago to bring Jacob to Joseph.

If that is correct, then the seven healthy ears of grain represent the greatest harvest of souls the world has ever known as it regards salvation.

I BELIEVE THE LORD TOLD ME THE FOLLOWING

This second part of Pharaoh's dream interpreted by Joseph is about to be fulfilled. I believe that He spoke to my heart that this ministry (Jimmy Swaggart Ministries) is going to play a great part in this move of God. I believe He also told me that this would be the last great worldwide move before the coming great tribulation. The potential is there for millions to be saved, and to be sure, the Lord can readily carry this out by the use of modern technology, and I speak of television, etc. I also believe that the Lord has told me that hundreds of thousands are going to be baptized with the Holy Spirit as well. It will be the greatest move of God regarding souls being saved, lives being changed, etc., the world has ever known.

I realize that the institutionalized church is in worse spiritual condition than at any time since the Reformation, but the Lord does not have to work through that particular effort. He can work outside of it and, in fact, will. Due to modern technology, and I speak of television and the Internet, it is possible to reach hundreds of millions of people with a single program or a single service.

PREPARATION STAGES

I believe we are now (2014) in the preparation stages. I have no idea as to how the Lord is going to bring all of this about regarding the entirety of the world, but I do know that

He has called this ministry (Jimmy Swaggart Ministries) for this particular purpose. I believe that He has promised me a greater moving of the Holy Spirit, which institutes a great anointing of the Holy Spirit, than we've ever previously known. That goes for everyone, and I mean everyone who prays for this ministry, who works for this ministry, who supports it financially, etc. This is one of the reasons our Media Church is so all-important. These are people from all over the world who have desired to be associated with Family Worship Center and are by means of television, the Internet, etc. It sobers one to realize that a dream that God gave a heathen monarch some 3,700 years ago and was interpreted by Joseph will have such a bearing on end-time events. However, I definitely believe that it was and it will.

ANCIENT HISTORY AND THE END TIME

So, when you read this book, you will be studying ancient history, and I speak of the fulfillment of events so startling as to boggle the mind. We also speak of coming world events, which will be the most important in history, and I speak of the salvation of millions of souls.

Of course, we know that God can do anything; however, the actual portent is staggering to say the least. My grandmother taught me many, many years ago when she said, *"Jimmy, God is a big God, so ask big."* I've never forgotten that. It has helped me to touch this world for Christ, and it will do so once again.

So, as you read these pages, I want you to do so with anticipation in mind. I want you to realize that as you read the Bible account of Joseph, you are reading something so absolutely stupendous that it defies description. There has never been one quite like Joseph. As stated, he was a type of Christ, and the way he dealt with his brothers is the way the Lord, in essence, will deal with Israel in a coming glad day. This will be at the second coming.

I realize that we who know the Lord know that nothing is impossible with Him. But yet, to read of events that took place some 3,700 years ago and how that much of it pertains to the end time, which is yet to come to pass, is startling indeed!

I personally feel this book will be of tremendous benefit to you as it regards understanding the Word of God a little better and, as well, end-time events which are right ahead of us.

> "Once our blessed Christ of beauty
> "Was veiled off from human view;
> "But through suffering death and sorrow
> "He has rent the veil in two."
>
> "Now, He is with God the Father,
> "Interceding there for you;
> "For He is the mighty conqueror
> "Since He rent the veil in two."

"Holy angels bow before Him,
"Men of earth give praises due;
"For He is the well-beloved,
"Since He rent the veil in two."

"Throughout time and endless ages,
"Heights and depths of love so true;
"He alone can be the giver,
"Since He rent the veil in two."

JOSEPH

JOSEPH'S BIRTH AND EARLY YEARS

JOSEPH'S BIRTH AND EARLY YEARS

"AND GOD REMEMBERED *Rachel, and God hearkened to her, and opened her womb.*

"And she conceived, and bore a son; and said, God has taken away my reproach:

"And she called his name Joseph; and said, The LORD *shall add to me another son"* (Gen. 30:22-24).

Ultimately God answered Rachel's petition and opened her womb.

As stated, she named her son Joseph, which means *"He shall add."* In effect, this was a prophecy referring to the birth of another son, who, in fact, would be Benjamin.

It seems by now that Rachel had advanced somewhat in the Spirit and had forsaken human devices, such as resorting to mandrakes. She now evidenced a complete dependence on the sovereign grace of the covenant God of Abraham, Isaac, and Jacob.

Concerning this, Stanley Horton says of her: *"When God remembers, it does not mean that He had forgotten. Rather it means that it was God's time and He actively entered the situation to do something about it. This intervention was to answer Rachel's prayers that He had been listening to the entire time of Leah's childbearing years. God, not the mandrakes, made it possible for Rachel to have a son. Barrenness was considered a disgrace. Now that disgrace was removed by the birth of a son. But she was not satisfied, since Leah had six sons. So she named the boy Joseph, meaning 'He shall add,' and she asked for another son. Unfortunately the fulfillment of that prayer would cause her death (Gen. 35:16-19)."*

Very little is said about Joseph regarding his upbringing.

When Jacob was to meet Esau, Joseph was mentioned. Concerning that time, the Scripture says, *"And he (Jacob) put the handmaids and their children foremost, and Leah and her children after, and Rachel and Joseph hindermost.*

"And he passed over before them, and bowed himself to the ground seven times, until he came near to his brother.

"And Esau ran to meet him, and embraced him, and fell on his neck, and kissed him: and they wept" (Gen. 33:2-4).

This occasioned Jacob with his family and herds coming back to the Promised Land. He had been away for more than 20 years. How old that Joseph was at this time, we aren't told; however, he was probably not much more than 4 or 5 years old. We now pick up with the account of his life when he was 17 years old as given to us in the Word of God.

The Scripture says: *"And Jacob dwelt in the land wherein his father was a stranger, in the land of Canaan.*

"These are the generations of Jacob. Joseph, being seventeen years old, was feeding the flock with his brethren; and the lad was with the sons of Bilhah, and with the sons of Zilpah, his father's wives: and Joseph brought unto his father their evil report" (Gen. 37:1-2).

Verse 2 sets Joseph forward as a shepherd 17 years of age. It is believed that his mother Rachel was still living but died within the year. It must be remembered that these accounts are not necessarily given in chronological order.

The story that is about to unfold before us is at least one of the most remarkable and one of the most powerful in the entirety of the Scriptures, and in history for that matter. It is a powerful testimony to the inspiration of the Word of God, for no man either before or after the writing of the New Testament could have composed such a story. As stated, it is one of the most remarkable in history.

Evidently Jacob's vast herds were divided into at least two flocks and perhaps even more. Joseph was with the sons of Bilhah and the sons of Zilpah, while the sons of Leah were evidently shepherding the other flock.

We aren't told exactly what the evil report was that Joseph related to his father, but it probably had to do with the immoral Canaanite practices in which his brothers were participating. There is some indication that he had first spoken to them about these practices, but that only aroused resentment against him in their hearts. While these men were in the covenant, so to speak, they were actually not a part of the covenant. In other words, they knew about God, but they really didn't know God.

THE COAT OF COLORS

"Now Israel loved Joseph more than all his children, because he was the son of his old age: and he made him a coat of many colors" (Gen. 37:3).

If it is to be noticed, the Holy Spirit used here the name Israel, signifying that what was done here regarding Joseph was totally of the Lord. Many have claimed that Jacob caused this problem among his sons by favoring Joseph. That's not true!

The love expressed here had to do with the Lord laying His hand on Joseph, while Jacob's other sons had rejected the Lord. Even though Jacob loved all of his sons, his love for Joseph had to do with the will of God. While he was his youngest (Benjamin having not yet been born), still, that was not the primary reason.

Because of sin on the part of his other sons, there was no fellowship between Jacob and these sons. In fact, there couldn't be any fellowship, as would be obvious. There was fellowship with Joseph because of the touch of God on his life, and above all, his love for God.

THE BIRTHRIGHT

The coat of many colors holds a special meaning. It was to be worn by the one who was to have the birthright, normally the firstborn. However, as it had been with Jacob and Esau, the firstborn, who was Reuben, would not have this position of leadership. The Holy Spirit proclaimed that it should go to

Joseph. When Jacob left this mortal coil, Joseph, in essence, was to be the high priest of the family, which the following years graphically proved to be the case!

Jacob didn't want to make the mistake his father Isaac had made. Isaac didn't want to give the birthright to Jacob even though the Lord had made it very plain at the birth of the two boys that this was to be the case. Jacob coming by that position as a result of Isaac's procrastination was fraught with difficulties and problems. Jacob was determined that this would not be the case with his actions. The moment the Lord told him that Joseph was to be the one, however that happened, Jacob immediately proclaimed his position by making Joseph this many-colored coat, which he would wear at certain times. As we shall see, none of this sat well at all with his brothers.

HATRED

"And when his brethren saw that their father loved him more than all his brethren, they hated him, and could not speak peaceably unto him" (Gen. 37:4).

This perfectly epitomizes Christ, of whom Joseph was one of the most remarkable types found in the Word of God. God loved His Son and showed it greatly by lavishing upon Him all the power of the Holy Spirit. As a result, the Jews, who were His brethren, so to speak, hated Him.

So, what we see here regarding this scenario is a perfect picture of Christ. This hatred — and hatred it is — follows down in the church regarding the same principles. What do I mean by that?

Those on whom the Lord has laid His hand will ultimately be hated by the church. As we have previously stated, this small family, which actually constituted the church of its day, had little trouble with its surrounding neighbors, although they were heathen. The greatest problems came from within, even as we are studying here. It is the same with the modern church. The hatred and animosity little comes from without, but rather from within.

THE DREAMS

"And Joseph dreamed a dream, and he told it his brethren: and they hated him yet the more.

"And he said unto them, Hear, I pray you, this dream which I have dreamed:

"For, behold, we were binding sheaves in the field, and, lo, my sheaf arose, and also stood upright; and, behold, your sheaves stood round about, and made obeisance to my sheaf.

"And his brethren said to him, Shall you indeed reign over us? or shall you indeed have dominion over us? And they hated him yet the more for his dreams, and for his words" (Gen. 37:5-8).

The Lord revealed the future to Joseph in a dream. While the dream definitely referred to him, with it ultimately being fulfilled, it more so referred to Christ and Israel. He told his brothers the truth, and they hated him even more. Thus it was with Joseph's great Antitype. He bore witness to the truth, and his testimony to the truth was answered on man's part by the Cross.

The mention of Joseph's mother in Verse 10 is thought by some to be a mistake in the sacred text, with Rachel already being dead. However, she was still living at the time and died shortly afterward. As stated, these accounts are not necessarily given in chronological order.

By looking at these dreams from the natural viewpoint, many have suggested that it was prideful arrogance that had Joseph to relate these dreams to his brothers. However, it was not done in pride since there is no reason to suppose that Joseph as yet understood the celestial origin of his dreams, much less what they meant.

A TYPE OF CHRIST

Concerning this, *The Pulpit Commentary* says: "*He related this in the simplicity of his heart and in doing so he was also guided, unconsciously it may be, but still really, by an overruling providence, who made use of the very telling of the dream as a step toward its fulfillment.*"

The Pulpit Commentary continues, "*In the absence of information to the contrary, we are warranted in believing that there was nothing either sinful or offensive in Joseph's spirit or manner in making known his dreams. That which appears to have excited the hostility of his brethren was not the mode of their communication, but the character of their contents.*"

In fact, due to the principle of Joseph being a type of Christ and, without a doubt, the most powerful type in the Old Testament, no sin whatsoever is recorded as it regards this brother. While he very definitely did commit sins at times simply because the Scripture says that *"all have sinned and come short of the glory of God,"* still, these sins were not recorded because of his place and position. To be sure, if what Joseph did in relating these dreams was wrong, the Holy Spirit would have said so or else ignored the incident.

While the dream definitely had to do with Joseph, as we shall see, Joseph's life and experiences far more portrayed Christ. Concerning the dream, while his brothers would definitely bow down to him, the greater meaning has to do with the time that is coming when Israel will bow down to Christ. This will take place immediately after the second coming. That is by far the greater meaning and that which the Holy Spirit intends to present.

THE TRUTH

The hatred that Joseph's brethren exhibited toward him represents the Jews in Christ's day. *"He came to His own, and His own received Him not."* He had *"no form nor come-liness"* in their eyes. They would not own Him as the Son of God or as the King of Israel. Their eyes were not open to behold *"His glory, the glory as of the Only Begotten of the Father, full of grace and truth."* They would not have Him. They hated Him.

REVELATION

"And he dreamed yet another dream, and told it his brethren, and said, Behold, I have dreamed a dream more; and behold, the sun and the moon and the eleven stars made obeisance to me.

"And he told it to his father, and to his brethren: and his father rebuked him, and said unto him, What is this dream that you have dreamed? Shall I and your mother and your brethren indeed come to bow down ourselves to you to the earth?

"And his brethren envied him; but his father observed the saying" (Gen. 37:9-11).

As it regards Joseph, we see that in no wise did he relax his testimony in consequence of his brothers' refusal of his first dream. He dreamed another dream and told it, as well, to his brethren and his father.

This was simple testimony founded upon divine revelation, but it was testimony that brought Joseph down to the pit. Had he kept back his testimony or taken off part of its edge and power, he might have spared himself, but no, he told them the truth, and, therefore, they hated him even more.

THE TESTIMONY OF CHRIST

Concerning this, C.H. Mackintosh said: *"Thus was it with Joseph's great Antitype. He bore witness to the truth — He witnessed a good confession — He kept back nothing — He could only speak of the truth because He was Truth, and His testimony to the truth was answered, on man's part by the Cross, the vinegar, the soldier's spear.*

"The testimony of Christ too, was connected with the deepest, fullest, richest grace. He not only came as 'The Truth,' but also as the perfect expression of all the love of the Father's heart: 'grace and truth came by Jesus Christ.' He was the full disclosure to man of what God was, and was the full disclosure to God of what man ought to have been, but was not; hence man was left entirely without excuse. He came and showed God to man, and man hated God with a perfect hatred. The fullest exhibition of divine love was answered by the fullest exhibition of human hatred. This is seen in the Cross; and we have it touchingly foreshadowed at the pit into which Joseph was cast by his brethren."

THE SENDING OF JOSEPH

"And his brethren went to feed their father's flock in Shechem.

"And Israel said unto Joseph, Do not your brethren feed the flock in Shechem? come, and I will send you unto them. And he said to him, Here am I.

"And he said to him, Go, I pray you, see whether it is well with your brethren, and well with the flocks; and bring me word again. So he sent him out of the vale of Hebron, and he came to Shechem" (Gen. 37:12-14).

Joseph was given more revelation through another dream. Little did all of these men know, even Joseph or his father, as to how important this revelation actually was.

In these dreams, the Holy Spirit portrayed Israel's acceptance of Christ when, in fact, at the time the dream was given, there was no Israel, at least as far as a nation was concerned.

The short phrase, *Here am I*, in reply to Jacob's request of Joseph, foreshadows the statement of Christ, *"Then said I, Lo, I come: in the volume of the book it is written of Me.*

"I delight to do Your will, O My God: Yes, Your law is within My heart" (Ps. 40:7-8).

The conspiracy against Joseph to murder him foreshadowed the conspiracy of the religious leaders of Israel to murder Christ.

Jacob sending Joseph to his brethren in order to find out how they were doing proves that he did not understand at all the depths of their hatred for Joseph. However, all of this foreshadowed God sending His Son, the Lord Jesus Christ, to the nation of Israel, even as Israel was raised up for this very purpose. The difference is, whereas Jacob was ignorant of the degree of hatred evidenced against Joseph, God was not ignorant at all but knew totally of the hatred on the part of Israel that would be evidenced toward Christ. Nevertheless, this did not deter Him at all!

"Marvelous grace of our loving Lord,
"Grace that exceeds our sin and our guilt,
"Yonder on Calvary's mount outpoured,
"There where the blood of the Lamb was spilt."

"Sin and despair like the sea waves cold,
"Threaten the soul with infinite loss;
"Grace that is greater, yes, grace untold,
"Points to the Refuge, the mighty Cross."

"Dark is the stain that we cannot hide,
"What can avail to wash it away?
"Look, there is flowing a crimson tide,
"Whiter than snow you may be today."

"Marvelous, infinite, matchless grace,
"Freely bestowed on all who believe;
"You that are longing to see His face,
"Will you this moment His grace receive?"

JOSEPH

CHAPTER

2

THE CONSPIRACY

CHAPTER TWO

THE CONSPIRACY

"AND A CERTAIN *man found him (found Joseph), and,*
behold, he was wandering in the field: and the man asked
him, saying, What do you seek?

"*And he said, I seek my brethren: tell me, I pray you,*
where they feed their flocks.

"*And the man said, They are departed from here; for I*
heard them say, Let us go to Dothan. And Joseph went after
his brethren, and found them in Dothan.

"*And when they saw him afar off, even before he came*
near unto them, they conspired against him to kill him"
(Gen. 37:15-18).

Little did Jacob realize that his sending Joseph to his
brothers would instigate a time of sorrow of unparalleled
proportions. It would break his heart to such an extent that,
in fact, there are no words that could adequately describe, at
least properly, what Joseph's brothers did to him and, thereby,
to their aged father Jacob.

Such is sin. It has no heart. It truly steals, kills, and destroys.

The sons of Jacob were guilty of murder, for their hatred fostered such. The Scripture plainly says that *"whosoever hates his brother is a murderer" (I Jn. 3:15)*, and this even though the deed itself may not be carried out.

The sons of Jacob hated their brother because their father loved him. Joseph was a type of Christ, for though He was the beloved Son of His Father and hated by a wicked world, yet the Father sent Him out of His bosom to visit us in great humility and love. He came from Heaven to earth to seek and save us, and that despite our hatred toward Him.

CHRIST IN THE ACTIONS OF JOSEPH

He came to His own, and His own not only received Him not but consulted saying, *"This is the Heir, come, let us kill Him; crucify Him, crucify Him!"* This He submitted to in pursuance of His design to redeem and save us.

As we go forward in this narrative, we will see Christ in the actions of Joseph set out perfectly before us. As such, we must learn what the Holy Spirit is telling us through the life of this man.

Dothan was about 12 miles north of Shechem, with Shechem being about 50 miles north of Hebron. So, Joseph would have to walk more than 60 miles to find his brothers.

Even before he arrived there, that is, when they saw him coming, they conspired to kill him. It was thus so with Christ as well. When He was born, Herod sought to kill Him (Mat., Chpt. 2).

SHECHEM?

If it is to be remembered, Shechem is the place where Simeon and Levi killed all the men of that small town because their sister Dinah had been raped.

Some period of time had now passed, but the greater reason that the brothers were not fearful of reprisal is probably due to their great strength.

That Jacob would have to send a part of his herds so far away as to Shechem — a distance of some 50 miles or more — tells us how large these herds were and, therefore, the power of Jacob. There is a possibility that there was quite a number of other men with the brothers at that time and, no doubt, were actually serving in their employ, which would have made this group powerful indeed.

REUBEN

"And they said one to another, Behold, this dreamer comes.

"Come now therefore, and let us kill him, and cast him into some pit, and we will say, Some evil beast has devoured him: and we shall see what will become of his dreams.

"And Reuben heard it, and he delivered him out of their hands; and said, Let us not kill him.

"And Reuben said unto them, Shed no blood, but cast him into this pit that is in the wilderness, and lay no hand upon him; that he might rid him out of their hands, to deliver him to his father again" (Gen. 37:19-22).

Partly through the personal character of Joseph, partly through the evil passions of his brethren, partly through the apparently casual incidents of the neighborhood, partly through the Spirit of righteousness working in the heart of Reuben, and partly through the weakness and fondness of Jacob, we see all things working together in God's hands! He wove the web composed of many single threads into one united, orderly pattern as a whole in which we are able to trace His own thought and purpose.

When we look at Joseph in the pit and in the prison, and look at him afterward as ruler over all the land of Egypt, we see the difference between the thoughts of God and the thoughts of men. So, when we look at the Cross and at the throne of the Majesty in the heavens, we see the same thing.

Nothing ever brought out the real state of man's heart toward God but the coming of Christ.

CONSCIENCE

Reuben was actually the firstborn; consequently, it was to him that the birthright should have gone. This would have guaranteed him a double portion of Jacob's riches when the patriarch came down to die. So, he would have had the most to gain from Joseph's death, who, by now, had been given the birthright instead. However, Reuben seemed to have some conscience left, where his brethren did not. As such, the Scripture says, *"He delivered him out of their hands; and said, Let us not kill him."*

Several things greatly rankled these men.

The dreams angered them greatly, as did the coat of many colors. So, they would kill the one who dreamed the dreams and strip the coat from him, thinking to silence his voice. Little did they know what the future held!

Reuben suggested that they put Joseph in a pit, which they did, with him thinking that he would come back later and rescue the boy. Evidently he had to go some place. When he returned, he found that Joseph was gone. They had sold him to the Ishmaelites.

Along with Reuben, Judah was the one who saved the life of Joseph, suggesting that they sell him as a slave. However, this was little an act of mercy on the part of Judah inasmuch as under normal circumstances, they were consigning him to a life worse than death.

TWENTY PIECES OF SILVER

"And it came to pass, when Joseph was come unto his brethren, that they stripped Joseph out of his coat, his coat of many colors that was on him;

"And they took him, and cast him into a pit: and the pit was empty, there was no water in it.

"And they sat down to eat bread: and they lifted up their eyes and looked, and, behold, a company of Ishmaelites came from Gilead with their camels bearing spicery and balm and myrrh, going to carry it down to Egypt.

"And Judah said unto his brethren, What profit is it if we kill our brother, and conceal his blood?

"Come, and let us sell him to the Ishmaelites, and let not our hand be upon him: for he is our brother and our flesh. And his brethren were content.

"Then there passed by Midianites merchantmen; and they drew and lifted up Joseph out of the pit, and sold Joseph to the Ishmaelites for twenty pieces of silver: and they brought Joseph into Egypt" (Gen. 37:23-28).

The merchants who bought Joseph were called both Midianites and Ishmaelites. They were sons of Abraham by Hagar and Keturah, making them kin in some distant way to the Israelites. These brothers sitting down to eat bread, even after they had thrown Joseph into the pit, shows how hard their hearts were, indicating deplorable brutality on their part. In their minds, they had satisfactorily disposed of the young man and his dreams. This coat of colors, which signified that he had now been chosen for the birthright instead of Reuben, would be used to deceive his father.

Evidently, when they put him in the pit, their idea was to let him starve to death, but now, a change of events came about in that they spotted a camel train coming near them and going down to Egypt. They would sell Joseph as a slave to these Ishmaelites and make some profit from the transaction. Judah was the one who suggested this. They would get 20 pieces of silver. This is a type of Christ being sold for 30 pieces of silver.

As they stripped the coat from Joseph, likewise, they cast lots for Jesus' robe.

THE DECEPTION

"And Reuben returned unto the pit; and, behold, Joseph was not in the pit; and he rent his clothes.

"And he returned unto his brethren, and said, The child is not; and I, where shall I go?

"And they took Joseph's coat, and killed a kid of the goats, and dipped the coat in the blood;

"And they sent the coat of many colors, and they brought it to their father; and said, This have we found: know now whether it be your son's coat or no.

"And he knew it, and said, It is my son's coat; an evil beast has devoured him; Joseph is without doubt rent in pieces" (Gen. 37:29-33).

The Scripture says they *"killed a kid of the goats"* and then dipped Joseph's coat in the blood. Rebekah used a kid of the goats to deceive Isaac as it regarded Jacob (Gen. 27:9).

Instead of taking the coat to Jacob, they evidently sent it by a slave and told the slave what to say. Joseph was sold as a slave into Egypt, and the brothers thought they would never see him again.

It seems that Reuben was genuinely sorry about the turn of events; however, they explained to him what they had done, and the record proclaims the fact that he did nothing further.

THE COAT

To be frank, Reuben could easily have overtaken the Ishmaelites and Midianites and bought Joseph back, but he made no effort to do so.

As stated, in order to deceive their father, they evidently got an employee or slave to take the bloody coat to Jacob and to give him the story they had concocted. More than likely, the slave didn't know the truth of the matter either. He would have, in all good conscience, related to Jacob what they told him to say.

This being the case, the slave would not have had any knowledge of this coat of many colors or that it had been given to Joseph by his father. The slave only knew what he had been told to say, so he handed Jacob the coat, with others probably with him, and asked Jacob if this coat actually belonged to Joseph.

Jacob recognized it immediately and then surmised what his evil sons wanted him to surmise — that a wild animal had killed Joseph.

Knowing how much Jacob loved Joseph, it seems that the brothers took some glee in the suffering they caused the patriarch at this time. However, even as the next two verses portray, his grief, it seems, was even greater than they had anticipated it would be. It almost killed the old man!

EGYPT

"And the Midianites sold him into Egypt unto Potiphar, an officer of Pharaoh's, and captain of the guard" (Gen. 37:36).

It is said that in those days the method for transporting slaves was to put each one in a wicker basket, where they would be placed in a cart or strapped to the side of a camel. This would keep them from escaping.

So, on his way to Egypt, Joseph would have passed very close to his home in Hebron, but he was powerless to say or do anything. Bottled up in this awkward setting and unable to stretch his legs, after awhile, the pain would have become excruciating. However, to be sure, those who had bought him little cared for his comfort, as would be obvious.

It is also obvious that the Lord was watching over him every mile of the way. Joseph being sold to Potiphar, the captain of Pharaoh's guard, was no accident. It was planned by the Lord.

A TYPE OF CHRIST

Considering that Joseph was a type of Christ and considering his righteous life, one may wonder why the Lord would submit him to such difficulties. Well, the same could be said for Jacob and untold millions of other believers down through the many centuries.

Faith must be tested, and great faith must be tested greatly. As it regards the child of God, every single thing with the believer, even as we have stated, is a test.

As should be obvious, this hardly matches up to the modern gospel being preached, claiming that proper faith will exempt one from all difficulties. No, it doesn't match up because the modern gospel is wrong.

THE MEASURING OF FAITH?

It is pathetic when one's faith is measured against the price of the suit he wears or the model of car he drives. How would such foolishness have stacked up with Joseph, or Jacob for that matter?

The Christian life, at least according to the Bible, doesn't claim a life exempt from all problems and difficulties. In fact, the Lord definitely allows certain adverse things to come our way in order for our faith to be tested.

When God blesses us, we learn about God and how wonderful and glorious that He is; however, we learn little about ourselves. It takes adversity, trouble, and difficulties for us to learn about ourselves, and most of the time, what we find is not very pleasant. So, the blessings teach us about God, while adversity teaches us about ourselves.

The last verse of Genesis, Chapter 37, says that Joseph was *"sold into Egypt."* As the story will tell, Joseph would become the second most powerful man in Egypt. As well, Jesus Christ would rise from the dead and become the head of the church, which is by and large also made up of Gentiles.

"And can it be that I should gain
"An interest in the Saviour's blood?
"Died He for me, who caused His pain?
"For me who Him in death pursued?"

"He left His Father's throne above,
"So free, so infinite His grace!
"Emptied Himself of all but love,
"And bled for Adam's helpless race."

"No condemnation now I dread,
"Jesus, and all in Him is mine;
"Alive in Him, my living Head,
"And clothed in righteousness divine."

JOSEPH

CHAPTER

3

JOSEPH IN EGYPT

CHAPTER THREE

JOSEPH IN EGYPT

"AND JOSEPH WAS brought down to Egypt; and Potiphar, an officer of Pharaoh, captain of the guard, an Egyptian, bought him of the hands of the Ishmaelites, which had brought him down thither" (Gen. 39:1).

We will find that some eight times in Chapter 39 of Genesis, in one way or another, it is said that the Lord was with Joseph. Eight speaks of resurrection, so it tells us that whatever happened with Joseph, no matter how adverse it seemed at the moment, a resurrection was coming.

In the story of Joseph, we will perceive a remarkable chain of events, all tending to one grand point, namely, the exaltation of the man who had been in the pit.

We will ultimately see that the leading object was to exalt the one whom men had rejected, and then to produce in those same men a sense of their sin as it regarded this rejection.

POTIPHAR

It is ironic that this young man, who was sold as a slave, would ultimately be the prime minister of Pharaoh, would save from starvation the patriarchal family, and finally, would see them settled in Goshen, a part of Egypt.

This is something that only God could do. It is done to portray Christ, for Joseph was a type of Christ and perhaps the most beautiful type of the entirety of the Old Testament. While studying his life, we will see Christ and what would ultimately happen to Christ. We will also see prophetic events that have not even yet come to pass but will do so shortly.

During the time of Joseph, it is believed that the Hyksos then ruled Egypt, having defeated the Egyptians in battle a short time earlier. This is the reason that Potiphar is identified as an Egyptian. This means it was somewhat unusual at that time for an Egyptian under the Hyksos to hold such a high position. It seems that the Hyksos ruled for about 100 years.

So now Joseph, who was about 17 or 18 years old, was sold by the Ishmaelites to Potiphar, the captain of the guard. All of this was being guided by the hand of the Lord, even down to the minute details.

THE BLESSINGS OF THE LORD

"And the LORD was with Joseph, and he was a prosperous man; and he was in the house of his master the Egyptian" (Gen. 39:2).

I want the reader to note that despite the fact that Joseph had been thrown into a pit, had been sold as a slave, and was now hundreds of miles from his home and family, not knowing if he would ever see them again, the Scripture emphatically states, *"And the* LORD *was with Joseph."* What a statement!

We find in all of these happenings that the finger of the Lord was guiding all the springs of the vast machine of circumstances, that nothing functions without His knowledge, and as it regards the Blood-bought redeemed, *"All things work together for good to them who love God, to them who are the called according to His purpose"* (Rom. 8:28).

Due to so much false teaching, if this scenario were set down in the 21st century, I doubt that many in the modern church would think that the Lord was with Joseph. However, He was! We are made to believe by false teaching that only that which outwardly looks like great blessings could be of the Lord. What has that teaching produced?

A PROSPEROUS MAN

For the most part, this modern teaching has produced spoiled Christian brats. However, if the Lord wants Army Rangers, Green Berets, or Navy SEALs — spiritually speaking of course — then they are going to have to undergo the same spiritual training as Joseph.

The Holy Spirit referred to him as a prosperous man, and yet, he was a slave. This means that even as a slave, everything that Joseph touched was blessed by God. So, this means that where he was (in this case, the house of the Egyptian), was blessed by God as well! Little did Potiphar know and realize just who Joseph was when he was purchased.

In fact, it would have been impossible for him to have put together the facts that Joseph was a slave and yet was blessed by God more so than any other human being in the world at that time. The questions that hang heavy over such a situation could not have been answered by Potiphar, or probably anyone else for that matter.

THE BLESSING

"And his master saw that the LORD was with him, and that the Lord made all that he did to prosper in his hand" (Gen. 39:3).

Potiphar had more sense than most Christians. He saw that the hand of the Lord was on Joseph and took advantage of that, even as he should have done.

It is strange. The world will oftentimes see the blessings of God upon an individual and recognize it as such, while the church far too often exhibits jealousy. Consequently, the work of God is greatly hindered by such action and attitudes.

GRACE

"And Joseph found grace in his (Potiphar's) sight, and he served him: and he made him (Joseph) overseer over his house, and all that he had he put into his hand" (Gen. 39:4).

This does not imply that Potiphar was acquainted with Jehovah, but simply that he concluded Joseph to be under divine protection.

Potiphar made Joseph the business manager over all of his holdings, whatever that might have been, which, no doubt, was considerable.

The circumstances of Joseph's lot might have induced despondency, indifference, inaction, carelessness, and inattention. However, divine grace so upheld and cheered him that he was able to go about his duties with joy and cheerfulness so that everything to which he turned his hand succeeded.

It is not our surroundings or circumstances which bring about happiness and joy. Unfortunately, the world thinks it does, but it doesn't! It is one's walk with the Lord, one's relationship with the Lord, and one's nearness to the Lord that makes a penitentiary into a palace, a hell into a heaven, and sadness into gladness. That's why the Scripture tells us, *"The joy of the LORD is your strength" (Neh. 8:10).* If you'll notice, it said, *"the joy of the LORD."* It is His joy, not ours, but it becomes ours when we have the proper relationship with Christ that we ought to have. Unfortunately, the world and even most of the church attempt to have joy without Christ. Such is not to be. He has the joy, and He will freely give it to us if we will walk exclusively with Him (Jn. 10:10).

MANY, MANY BLESSINGS

"And it came to pass from the time that he (Potiphar) had made him (Joseph) overseer in his house, and over all that he had, that the LORD blessed the Egyptian's house for

Joseph's sake; and the blessing of the LORD *was upon all that he had in the house, and in the field.*

"And he left all that he had in Joseph's hand; and he knew not ought he had, save the bread which he did eat. And Joseph was a goodly person, and well favored" (Gen. 39:5-6).

If it is to be noticed, the Scripture says that the blessing came *"for Joseph's sake."*

With Joseph being a type of Christ, this means that the blessings given by God the Father, who has all good things, comes upon us for *Jesus' sake.*

We must realize and have it penetrate our hearts and lives that all that Jesus did was done exclusively for us. This knowledge must remain in our hearts and lives permanently. Of all the things He did, not one of them was done for Heaven, angels, God the Father, or Himself. Everything was done exclusively for us. Therefore, all that He did carries an eternal meaning, which we must come to know.

We must know and understand that Jesus is God, has always been God, and will always be God. As God, He had no beginning and was not formed, made, created, or born. He always has been, always is, and always shall be.

THE INCARNATION

However, He became man, with Paul referring to Him as *"the last Adam"* and *"the second man"* (*I Cor. 15:45-47*).

The term, *the last Adam,* was used because there will never be the need for another one.

The phrase, the second man, was used in this fashion because the Lord is making many, many men in the image of Christ. Consequently, one might say, *"the third man,"* or *"the millionth man."* In fact, God originally intended for husband and wife to bring children of God into the world. However, due to Adam's fall, only in the likeness of Adam can babies be brought forth, hence, all the trouble and heartache in the world today. It is called *original sin.* Soon that will change!

Even though becoming a man, Jesus was a man as there has never been a man. Born of the Virgin Mary, He was born without original sin and, in fact, had no sin nature.

As Jesus, the Son of God, He kept the Law perfectly in every respect, all on our behalf. This perfect, ideal man never failed even one single time in all that He did. Again I emphasize that this was done all on our behalf, actually, as our substitute. So, this means that what He did was far more than simply doing it for us. In reality, He was the substitute man, doing for us what we could not do for ourselves.

After He had kept the Law perfectly all on our behalf, He then went to the Cross, which was planned from before the ages (I Pet. 1:18-20). Therefore, the Cross was to atone for all sin — past, present, and future — at least for all who will believe (Jn. 1:29; 3:16).

Atoning for all sin, Satan had no way or means to hold Jesus in the death world. Jesus rose from the dead; however, the entirety of the Cross — exactly as His life — was all for us. Therefore, when the believing sinner comes to Christ, in the mind of God, we are baptized into His death (Rom. 6:3-5).

BAPTIZED INTO HIS DEATH

Now, this is not speaking of water baptism as many believe, but rather the crucifixion of Christ. The word *baptized* was used by the Holy Spirit through Paul in order to impress upon us the totality of what happened to us when we came to Christ. We are literally placed *"in Christ"* (Rom. 8:1).

As well, the word baptized can be used figuratively or literally. Paul was using it figuratively. John the Baptist, using the word baptized both figuratively and literally, said, *"I indeed baptize you with water* (literally) *... but He who comes after me is mightier than I ... He shall baptize you* (used figuratively) *with the Holy Spirit and with fire"* (Mat. 3:11).

All of this means that while we died with Christ, we were also buried with Him. This means that all that we once were — and I speak of the sin, degradation, bondage, and iniquity — was buried with Him. We died when Christ died (Rom. 6:7-8), but it doesn't stop there; we were then raised with Him in newness of life, which speaks of the born-again experience (Jn. 3:3, 16).

Understanding all of this, our faith is then to forever rest in Christ and what He did for us in His sufferings. We are to reckon ourselves *"to be dead indeed unto sin* (the sin nature), *but alive unto God, through Jesus Christ our Lord"* (Rom. 6:11).

Continuing to exhibit faith in Christ and what He did for us at the Cross, and forever continuing in that capacity, we can be assured that *"sin shall not have dominion over you:*

for you are not under the Law (Jesus having satisfied that demand)*, but under grace"* (Rom. 6:14).

So, for Jesus' sake, God the Father gives us all things. However, we must always remember that all of these great and glorious things come to us exclusively by and through what Jesus did for us at the Cross. As we've said repeatedly, Christ and the Cross must never be divided. Jesus without the Cross is actually *"another Jesus"* (II Cor. 11:4). All blessings, all victory, and all grace, in fact, everything, comes to us for Jesus' sake.

EVERYTHING IS IN JESUS

Genesis 39:6 says, *"And he left all that he had in Joseph's hand."* Of course, this is speaking of Potiphar; however, Joseph being a type of Christ, it means that the Father has put everything into the hands of Christ. Of this, Jesus said, *"All things that the Father has are Mine"* (Jn. 16:15).

So, individuals who think that one can be saved and go to Heaven by worshipping and serving Muhammad, Buddha, etc., simply don't know what they're talking about. The Father has given nothing to these imposters, only to Jesus. In fact, and as stated, He has given everything to Christ. Once again, this was done because of what Jesus did at the Cross as it regards this great redemption plan.

As well, when it says in Verse 6, *"And Joseph was a goodly person, and well favored,"* the same can be said of Christ. In fact, it is of Jesus alone that the Father has said, *"This is My beloved Son, in whom I am well pleased"* (Mat. 3:17). If it is to be noticed, the Lord is pleased only with Christ, and for all the obvious reasons. So, for Him to be pleased with us, this can only be said and done providing we are in Christ.

This is the reason that we must carefully do our best to understand Christ, and to always place our faith squarely in Him and what He did for us in the sacrifice of Himself on the Cross.

> *"That God should love a sinner such as I*
> *"Should yearn to change my sorrow into bliss,*
> *"Nor rest till He had planned to bring me nigh,*
> *"How wonderful is love like this!"*

> *"That Christ should join so freely in the scheme,*
> *"Although it meant His death on Calvary,*
> *"Did ever human tongue find nobler theme*
> *"Than love divine that ransomed me?"*

> *"That for a willful outcast such as I,*
> *"The Father planned, the Saviour bled and died;*
> *"Redemption for a worthless slave to buy,*
> *"Who long had law and grace defied."*

> *"And now He takes me to His heart—a son,*
> *"He asks me not to fill a servant's place;*
> *"The far-off country wanderings all are done,*
> *"Wide open are His arms of grace."*

JOSEPH

CHAPTER

4

TEMPTATION

CHAPTER FOUR

TEMPTATION

"And it came to pass after these things, that his master's wife cast her eyes upon Joseph, and she said, Lie with me" (Gen. 39:7).

Satan now instituted a very telling temptation against Joseph, and the Lord gave him certain latitude to do so. As we have stated, faith must be tested, and great faith must be tested greatly.

At times the Lord does the testing personally, and at times He uses other things — even Satan, as noted here. While the Lord does not tempt anyone, He does give Satan permission to tempt, as should be obvious.

It is said that Joseph was one of the most handsome young men of his day. In fact, it is stated that his attractiveness was celebrated all over the East. Persian poets of Sura 12 of the Koran speak of his beauty as perfect.

Tradition says that Zuleika, Potiphar's wife, was at first the most virtuous of women, but when she saw Joseph, she was so affected that she lost all self-control and became a slave to her passions.

On one occasion, she supposedly made a dinner and invited 40 of the most beautiful women in Egypt, who, when they saw Joseph, were so moved with admiration that they exclaimed with one accord that he must be an angel.

HOW TO HANDLE TEMPTATION

"But he refused, and said unto his master's wife, Behold, my master trusts me with all that is in the house, and he has committed all that he has to my hand" (Gen. 39:8).

Joseph refused the woman's advances, even though the temptation was great. He gave the reasons, which we will deal with a little later.

As the Bible student knows, Joseph's understanding of the ways of the Lord was that which his father Jacob had taught him. There was no Bible in those days, that first coming with Moses, with him writing the first five books of the Bible approximately 250 years later.

As well, as it regards the knowledge of the Lord at that particular time, the knowledge of Joseph, as well as the few others who then lived for the Lord, was wrapped up in the sacrificial system. The head of the house was to act as the priest of the home by offering up sacrifices, with the Lord having given those directions to Adam and Eve and it being passed down (Gen., Chpt. 4). I think it is obvious that they knew what the sacrifices represented, which was the Redeemer who was to come into this world, and who would die for lost humanity. This latter part was made clear to Abraham when he was told to offer up Isaac, with the Lord staying his hand at the last moment.

FAITH IN CHRIST AND THE CROSS

From Abraham, this information went to Isaac, then to Jacob, with Jacob giving it to his sons, of whom it seems Joseph was the only one who heeded, at least at that particular time.

Considering that Joseph was now a slave of Potiphar, it is doubtful that he was able to offer up sacrifices at that particular time, although that would more than likely change in the near future with the change of his status.

The point I'm attempting to make is Joseph had placed his faith entirely in Christ and what Christ would do at the Cross to the degree that he then understood the great plan of God. This means that Joseph escaped this temptation in the same manner in which we escape temptation presently. How is that?

While Joseph definitely refused the advances of this woman, he was able to refuse only by the help of God. Left to himself, I doubt very seriously that he would have passed this test.

The believer faces temptation presently by exhibiting faith in Christ and what Christ has done for us at the Cross. The only answer for sin is the Cross of Christ. This is so important that I ask you to please allow me to say it again: *There is no answer for sin except the Cross of Christ* (Rom. 6:1-14; 8:1-11; I Cor. 1:17, 18, 23; 2:2; Gal. 6:14; Col. 2:10-15).

The believer faces temptation presently by exhibiting faith in Christ and what Christ has done for us at the Cross. Unfortunately, most of the modern church has the idea that once a person is saved, he then has the power (willpower) to say no to sin.

If the believer is functioning in that capacity, after awhile, he is going to say yes to sin because that is not God's way. In other words, it has nothing to do with one's super willpower (Rom. 7:18).

While the *will* is definitely important, it is that we will subscribe to God's prescribed order. What is that?

John said, *"This is the victory that overcomes the world, even our faith"* (I Jn. 5:4). It is not willpower; it is faith.

WHAT DO WE MEAN BY THE WORD *FAITH*?

Most Christians instantly think they know what the meaning of faith is; however, the truth is, most don't.

The faith of which John spoke here, and which Paul addressed constantly, refers to faith in Christ and what Christ did at the Cross all on our behalf. When we speak of the Cross, we aren't speaking of the wooden beam on which Jesus died, but rather what Jesus there accomplished.

As we have already stated several times, faith in Christ and His substitutionary work on the Cross is the only kind of faith that God will recognize. While other types of faith may in truth be faith, it's not that which spends in the economy of the kingdom of Heaven.

When the believer places his faith totally and completely in Christ and what Christ has done for us in His sufferings, Satan will continue to tempt. However, the Holy Spirit, who is God, and who lives within the heart and life of the believer (I Cor. 3:16), will then greatly help the believer. The temptation is then overcome because the believer is not attempting to do this within himself, but all in Christ.

Now, this sounds very simple, but it's not simple at all. Satan will fight us on this ground more so than he will fight us in any other capacity. That's why Paul referred to this as *"the good fight of faith"* (I Tim. 6:12). Actually, this is the only fight in which we are called upon to engage.

We aren't really to fight sin, that already having been fought and won by the Lord Jesus Christ in His life and especially His death on the Cross of Calvary. Satan doesn't mind at all our expending our efforts on something that's already been done. However, when we place our faith in Christ and what Christ has done for us at the Cross, understanding that the Cross of Christ is the means by which all these good things are given to us, that's when Satan will do everything within his power to hinder. That's where the fight comes in, and a fight it is! If we try to overcome sin in any other way, we will fail.

WAR

I do not want the reader to think that even though his faith is correct, meaning that it's in Christ and the Cross exclusively, he will then have no more problem with Satan. That is wrong! This is war, and actually, Paul labeled it as *"warfare."*

The Holy Spirit through him said: **"(For the weapons of our warfare are not carnal** *(carnal weapons consist of those which are man-devised)*, **but mighty through God** *(the Cross of Christ [I Cor. 1:18])* **to the pulling down of strongholds;**

"Casting down imaginations *(philosophic strongholds; every effort man makes outside of the Cross of Christ)*, **and every high thing that exalts itself against the knowledge of God** *(all the pride of the human heart)*, **and bringing into captivity every thought to the obedience of Christ** *(can be done only by the believer looking exclusively to the Cross, where all victory is found; the Holy Spirit will then perform the task)"* **(II Cor. 10:4-5).**

Once again I call your attention to the fact that the Holy Spirit constantly referred to this situation we face as war. So, don't think that because you understand Christ and the Message of the Cross temptation ceases and Satan goes elsewhere. Not so! To be perfectly honest, even though we understand this that Paul gave us and are doing our very best to adhere strictly to what the Holy Spirit has stated, still, it's not going to be easy, as it is never easy. That's why the Holy Spirit through the apostle referred to it as war and warfare. In fact, the flesh is so dominant in the believer that it is easy to drift over into the flesh, thinking it is the Spirit. To be frank, the flesh can be very religious, and that deceives us. Of course, as we've already stated, the flesh, as Paul used the term, refers to the ability, motivation, education, knowledge, strength, efforts, talents, etc., of the human being. Within themselves, these things aren't wrong, but where the wrong comes in is where we try to live for God by these methods. This is something that cannot be done.

WHY IS IT THAT THE FLESH IS INSUFFICIENT?

Paul gives us the answer to that as well. He said:

"**And if Christ be in you** (*He is in you through the power and person of the Spirit [Gal. 2:20]*), **the body is dead because of sin** (*means that the physical body has been rendered helpless because of the Fall; consequently, the believer trying to overcome by willpower presents a fruitless task*); **but the Spirit** (*Holy Spirit*) **is life because of righteousness** (*only the Holy Spirit can make us what we ought to be, which means we cannot do it ourselves; once again, He performs all that He does within the confines of the finished work of Christ, i.e., 'the Cross'*)" (Rom. 8:10).

Then the Holy Spirit through Paul said: "**But if the Spirit** (*Holy Spirit*) **of Him** (*from God*) **Who raised up Jesus from the dead dwell in you** (*and He definitely does, that is, if you are saved*), **He who raised up Christ from the dead shall also quicken your mortal bodies** (*give us power in our mortal bodies that we might live a victorious life*) **by His Spirit Who dwells in you** (*we have the same power in us, through the Spirit, that raised Christ from the dead, and is available to us only on the premise of the Cross and our faith in that sacrifice*) (Rom. 8:11).

THE CROSS IS GOD'S WAY

As we've already stated, the Cross of Christ is God's way of dealing with sin. He has no other way because no other way is needed.

The Cross of Christ is something that took place nearly 2,000 years ago but has a continuing effect and, in fact, an effect that will never be discontinued. In other words, what Jesus did for us at the Cross is just as potent and available now as it was 15 minutes after He died on that wooden beam.

The following is a short article that someone sent me. It was not identified, meaning that no name was attached, so it's impossible for me to give the credit to whoever wrote this short message. It is to the point, and I think one of the greatest statements regarding the Cross that has been made in a long time.

THE COLLISION OF GOD AND SIN

"The Cross of Christ is the revealed truth of God's judgment on sin. Never associate the idea of martyrdom with the Cross of Christ. It was the supreme triumph, and it shook the very foundations of Hell. There is nothing in time or eternity more certain or irrefutable than what Jesus Christ accomplished on the Cross — He made it possible for the entire human race to be brought back into a right standing relationship with God. He made redemption the foundation of human life; that is, He made a way for every person to have fellowship with God."

HE CAME TO DIE

"The Cross was not something that just happened to Jesus — He came to die; the Cross was His purpose in coming. He is 'the Lamb slain from the foundation of the world' (Rev. 13:8). The Incarnation of Christ would have no meaning without the Cross. Beware of separating 'God was manifested in the flesh' from 'He made Him to be sin for us' (I Tim. 3:16; II Cor. 5:21). The purpose of the Incarnation was redemption. God came in the flesh to take sin away, not to accomplish something for Himself. The Cross is the central event in time and eternity and the answer to all the problems of both."

THE CROSS OF GOD

"The Cross is not the Cross of a man, but the Cross of God, and it can never be fully comprehended through human experience. The Cross is God exhibiting His nature. It is the gate through which any and every individual can enter into oneness with God. But it is not a gate we pass right through; it is one where we abide in the life that is found there.

"The heart of salvation is the Cross of Christ. The reason salvation is so easy to obtain is that is cost God so much. The Cross was the place where God and sinful man merged with a tremendous collision where the way of life was opened. But all the cost and pain of the collision was absorbed by the heart of God."

ISN'T THE RESURRECTION IMPORTANT?

Of course, it is! There is nothing that Jesus did that was not of supreme significance. However, it must be understood that the Cross did not depend on the Resurrection, but rather that the Resurrection depended on the Cross. In other words, if Jesus atoned for all sin at the Cross and overcame Satan and all his cohorts of darkness at the Cross, then the Resurrection was a given. However, if Jesus had failed to atone for even one sin, He could not have risen from the dead. Everything depended on the Cross.

That's the reason that the great veil that hid the Holy of Holies from the Holy Place was rent from top to bottom at the moment Jesus died. It did not await the Resurrection, the Ascension, or the Exaltation, but was ripped asunder by God the moment that Jesus *"yielded up the ghost"* (Mat. 27:50-51).

Josephus said that veil stood some 30 feet high, was two inches thick, and four yoke of oxen could not pull it apart. However, God ripped it from the top to the bottom, stipulating that now the way was open for man to come and *"take of the water of life freely"* (Rev. 22:17). It was the Cross of Christ that opened that door, which will remain open forever and forever. The Cross of Christ is the means by which every good thing is given to us from God. Without the Cross, there is no salvation! Without the Cross, there is no sanctification for the saint! Without the Cross, there is no healing! Without the Cross, there is no fellowship with God! Without the Cross, there is no forgiveness! Without the Cross, there is no grace and mercy!

SIN

"There is none greater in this house than I; neither has he kept back anything from me but you, because you are his wife: how then can I do this great wickedness, and sin against God?" (Gen. 39:9).

All sin is against God. Joseph referred to the suggestions of this woman as *"this great wickedness."*

Adultery is wrong in any capacity, and even though the commandment against this sin had not yet been given, the moral law had already been placed in the hearts of those few who truly followed the Lord.

In all of this we see that Joseph felt a keen responsibility toward his master, which he certainly should have, and more than all, toward God. To do such a thing that was suggested of him, he would be greatly betraying the man who had given him this great position of responsibility, which is a grievous sin. Above all, he would be sinning against God. The moral is, if we treat the Lord right, it is certain that we will treat our fellowman right.

CONTINUING TEMPTATION

And it came to pass, as she spoke to Joseph day by day, that he hearkened not unto her, to lie by her, or to be with her" (Gen. 39:10).

Unfortunately, Joseph's business repeatedly took him into the main house, which he could not avoid. At the same time, Potiphar's wife, knowing all off this, would lie in wait for Joseph. So, it was a continuing temptation pressed upon him day by day, with him continuing to resist.

The lengths to which she went, we can only imagine. However, one can be very certain that the temptation increased day by day, which means that it took the grace of God, exceedingly so, in order for Joseph to come out victorious each day. One can well imagine that Joseph greatly dreaded each day, knowing what he would face.

THE GARMENT

"And it came to pass about this time, that Joseph went into the house to do his business; and there was none of the men of the house there within.

"And she caught him by his garment, saying, Lie with me: and he left his garment in her hand, and fled, and got him out.

"And it came to pass, when she saw that he had left his garment in her hand, and was fled forth,

"That she called unto the men of her house, and spoke unto them, saying, See, he has brought in an Hebrew unto us to mock us; he came in unto me to lie with me, and I cried with a loud voice:

"And it came to pass, when he heard that I lifted up my voice and cried, that he left his garment with me, and fled, and got him out.

"And she laid up his garment by her, until his lord came home" (Gen. 39:11-16).

Of all of this, it is very obvious as to what happened.

Matthew Henry said: *"Chaste and holy love will continue, though slighted; but sinful love is easily changed into sinful hatred. Those who have broken the bonds of modesty will never be held by the bonds of truth."*

Evaluating Joseph, some would claim that after advances had been made, he should not have gone back into the house; however, as stated, of this, he had no choice. His business demanded that he frequent the place. It is certain that he would have done anything to have avoided contact with this woman, but the situation actually presented itself as a trap. So the trap was ultimately sprung.

The Devil would surmise that if he could not get Joseph to do that which was wrong, he would have him locked up in prison for years. Now, of course, the Lord could have stopped all of this, but the remainder of the chapter tells us why not!

THE HEBREW SERVANT

"And she spoke unto him according to these words, saying, The Hebrew servant, which you have brought unto us, came in unto me to mock me:

"And it came to pass, as I lifted up my voice and cried, that he left his garment with me, and fled out.

"And it came to pass, when his master heard the words of his wife, which she spoke unto him, saying, After this manner did your servant to me; that his anger was kindled" (Gen. 39:17-19).

The believer must understand that everything that happens to him is either caused by the Lord or allowed by the Lord. Now, we know and realize that the Lord did not cause this woman to do what she did, but it is evident that He did allow it.

Why?

Among other things, Joseph was being prepared for something. In fact, he was being prepared for the second most powerful position in the world, the prime minister, so to speak, of the greatest nation at that time on the face of the earth.

Of course, he knew not at all of such plans, but the point is this: he trusted God. He didn't know why the situation had been allowed to play out in this manner. No doubt, he asked himself the question many times, *"What did I do that would warrant such?"*

The answer is simple: Joseph didn't do anything that was wrong or negative, but yet, he was about to undergo several years of various severe circumstances.

THE LORD WAS WITH JOSEPH

"And Joseph's master took him, and put him into the prison, a place where the king's prisoners were bound: and he was there in the prison.

"But the LORD was with Joseph, and showed him mercy, and gave him favor in the sight of the keeper of the prison.

"And the keeper of the prison committed to Joseph's hand all the prisoners who were in the prison; and whatsoever they did there, he was the doer of it.

"The keeper of the prison looked not to anything that was under his hand; because the LORD *was with him, and that which he did, the* LORD *made it to prosper"* (Gen. 39:20-23).

Whereas Potiphar once had the best business manager he had ever known, the keeper of the prison now had the best jailer he had ever known.

We know that it was the will of God for Joseph to be placed in this prison, for Verse 21 says, *"But the* LORD *was with Joseph."* It is speaking of the Lord being with Joseph as it regarded grace, mercy, power, leading, and guidance — in a word, all things. While the Lord most definitely might be with someone who is out of the will of God or lacking in faith, at the same time, He definitely is not with them in this capacity.

THE WORD OF GOD

The Scripture further says of this event: *"He sent a man before them, even Joseph, who was sold for a servant:*

"Whose feet they hurt with fetters: he was laid in iron:

"Until the time that His Word came: the Word of the LORD *tried him.*

"The king sent and loosed him; even the ruler of the people, and let him go free.

"He made him lord of his house, and ruler of all his substance:

"To bind his princes at his pleasure; and teach his senators wisdom" (Ps. 105:17-22).

There is something else that must be considered in all of this: Considering the advances of this woman, the Lord may have done Joseph the greatest favor by having him put in prison. Joseph, despite being a type of Christ, was human as all other men. Considering his attractiveness, as to exactly how long he could have withstood such temptation is anyone's guess. We would like to think that he would have stood it indefinitely; however, I'm not so sure that would have been the case.

THE WAYS OF THE LORD

Then again, whatever part the seduction played to prepare Joseph for the task ahead, the Lord would have to put Jacob's son through an extremely arduous course. As stated, the Lord was with him in the prison just as much as He had been with him in the palace.

However, if Joseph had grown bitter, without a shadow of a doubt this would have greatly hindered the blessings of the Lord on the future prime minister.

Let us say it again: Due to the great price that was paid for us and the fact that we are not our own, but we belong entirely to the Lord, everything that happens to the believer is either caused by the Lord or allowed by the Lord. Satan doesn't have free rein whatsoever with any believer, even the weakest. In fact, he must ask permission from the Lord no matter what he does and no matter the degree that it is done (Job, Chpts. 1-2).

So, if, in fact, we have done something wrong (which Joseph didn't), we should realize that we deserve what is happening, and, in fact, we deserve much worse. At the same time, we must learn the lesson that the Lord is thereby teaching us, for He is always teaching us because everything to the child of God is a test.

"Saved by the blood of the Crucified One!
"Now ransomed from sin and a new work begun,
"Sing praise to the Father and praise to the Son,
"Saved by the blood of the Crucified One!"

"Saved by the blood of the Crucified One!
"The angels rejoicing because it is done;
"A child of the Father, joint heir with the Son,
"Saved by the blood of the Crucified One!"

"Saved by the blood of the Crucified One!
"The Father He spoke, and His will it was done;
"Great price of my pardon, His own precious Son;
"Saved by the blood of the Crucified One!"

"Saved by the blood of the Crucified One!
"All hail to the Father, all hail to the Son,
"All hail to the Spirit, the great Three in One!
"Saved by the blood of the Crucified One!"

JOSEPH

CHAPTER

5

THE BUTLER AND THE BAKER

CHAPTER FIVE

THE BUTLER AND THE BAKER

"And it came to pass after these things, that the butler of the king of Egypt and his baker had offended their lord the king of Egypt.

"And Pharaoh was angry against two of his officers, against the chief of the butlers, and against the chief of the bakers.

"And he put them in ward in the house of the captain of the guard, into the prison, the place where Joseph was bound" (Gen. 40:1-3).

One very gracious feature in Joseph's character was that he never murmured or complained. Another yet more beautiful one was his unselfish interests in the needs and sorrows of others, which, to say the least, is Christlike.

As we shall see, we will find the hand of the Lord in these proceedings. While the butler would not remember Joseph and do what he should have done, as we shall later see, he would be used as the instrument to make Joseph known to Pharaoh at a very critical time.

It is remarkable to observe the hand of God in all of this. We would do well to look at our own lives accordingly. Whatever it might be, whether good or seemingly bad, we must realize that we belong to Him and that He is moving events and people to a particular destination all on our behalf. To properly know and understand this should bring great comfort to the heart of the believer.

It is only the unredeemed who rage as *"waves of the sea, foaming out their own shame; wandering stars, to whom is reserved the blackness of darkness forever"* (Jude, Vs. 13).

To the contrary, the believer has the sure hand of the Lord constantly guiding him. The knowledge of the Lord is expended on our behalf. If we can see that, understand that, and, thereby, place our faith and confidence in that, knowing that it's all for our good, then whatever comes, it can be a blessing. This was true for Joseph, even though it was a prison in which he found himself through no fault of his own.

THE DREAM

"And the captain of the guard charged Joseph with them, and he served them: and they continued a season in ward.

"And they dreamed a dream both of them, each man his dream in one night, each man according to the interpretation of his dream, the butler and the baker of the king of Egypt, which were bound in the prison.

"And Joseph came in unto them in the morning, and looked upon them, and, behold, they were sad" (Gen. 40:4-6).

In studying the Word of God, it will become obvious that quite often the Lord uses dreams to carry forth His work in some way.

Concerning these dreams had by the butler and the baker, as the events proved, the interpretation put on them by Joseph showed the dreams to be no vague hallucinations of the mind, but divinely-sent foreshadowing of the future fortunes of the dreamers, whether good or bad.

As one can see, the Lord was working in all of these situations in order to bring about His desired will. Of course, the will of the Lord being brought about was predicated on the obedience of Joseph in all things. In fact, he was the only one who fell into this situation simply because he was the only one serving God. The others knew nothing about the Lord; therefore, whatever it was they did, whether good or bad, had little effect on the outcome as it regarded the things the Lord desired to do.

THE LORD WORKS ...

Let the believer understand the things that we are saying. While the Lord works with and through the unredeemed, as is obvious here, it is through believers that His ultimate purpose is carried out. That's the reason that Jesus said, *"You are the salt of the earth ... You are the light of the world"* (Mat. 5:13-14).

In other words, in all of Egypt, for all of its knowledge, riches, etc., the only light in that land was that provided by Joseph. Before he came, there was no light. By use of the word *light,* we're speaking of correct spiritual illumination that shows the right way in all things.

The more true believers there are in any given place, the more of this light that is present.

Please observe the nations of the world that know God and those that don't. First of all, look at those that do not espouse Christianity, but rather some other religion. Poverty and ignorance grip these poor, unfortunate people, with them little realizing that it's their religion that is the cause of this consternation.

ISLAM

For instance, let's look at Islam!

Anyway that you look at this religion, it has produced nothing but a failed culture in every capacity. There is no such thing as the separation of church and state in the Islamic religion. This particular religion is the government and rules everything, even down to the minute details of one's life.

The point I'm making is this: considering that the religion of Islam has total sway in the countries where it rules, there is no excuse for its failures.

However, the truth is the following: as stated, Islam has produced nothing but a failed culture in every single country over which it has authority. The culture has failed in every capacity, be it education, freedom, prosperity, quality of life, etc. In fact, the nations of the world that boast of Islam are some of, if not the poorest, on the face of the earth.

Take Saudi Arabia for instance: it is at least one of the richest of the Muslim nations because of the United States purchasing billions of dollars worth of oil from this government. However, even in that country, illiteracy is rampant, with the average income only approximately $1,600 per capita, while it's over $50,000 in the United States.

Looking at freedom for its people — and this goes for all Muslim countries — women are treated as little more than slaves. They have no rights, no freedoms, and are second-class citizens in every respect.

Even in countries where religion is not so oppressive — such as China where Buddhism and Confucianism reign, or India where Hinduism is supreme — the poverty and/or lack of freedom are rampant.

Even though the political pundits wouldn't admit it, the secret of the prosperity of the United States is not its form of government, its institutions of higher learning, or its industry. Rather, it is its worship of the Lord Jesus Christ, which provides light and illumination for all of these other things to be done.

Regrettably, our nation is losing its freedoms because of its rejection of the Word of God.

CHRISTIANITY

No, this is not an effort to make Christianity the state church. God forbid! In fact, no worse thing could be done than that. However, even though the separation of church and state is one of the cornerstones of this democracy, that doesn't mean the separation of God and state, and that's exactly what I think powerful voices in government are trying to do.

Whether our educators realize it or not, the entire fabric of proper education in this nation rests upon the Word of God. The moral tone of all that is right or wrong likewise rests upon these principles. In other words, the Word of God is the seedbed of the Constitution of this nation, as well as the Bill of Rights. As someone has well said, *"Much Bible, much freedom; little Bible, little freedom; no Bible, no freedom."*

Think about the following: almost all of the inventions that have brought the world into the modern technological age have been brought about since the turn of the 20th century. As well, I would dare say that 90 percent of all technological advancement has had its beginning in the United States. Also, this country can probably boast the largest number of born-again, Spirit-filled believers on the face of the earth, with the exception possibly of Brazil. My contention is, with the mighty outpouring of the Holy Spirit comes even more light and illumination in every capacity, whether spiritual or otherwise. Yes, that's what I'm saying!

The technological advancement of the world during these modern times can be linked to the outpouring of the Holy Spirit and the fulfillment of the prophecy of Daniel. The Lord spoke to the great prophet–statesman and said, *"But you, O Daniel, shut up the words, and seal the book even to the time of the end: many shall run to and fro, and knowledge shall be increased"* (Dan. 12:4).

Technology and knowledge of the Word of God have both increased in these last of the last days exactly as prophesied by Daniel.

THE INTERPRETATION

"And he asked Pharaoh's officers who were with him in the ward of his lord's house, saying, Why do you look so sad today?

"And they said unto him, We have dreamed a dream, and there is no interpreter of it. And Joseph said unto them, Do not interpretations belong to God? tell me them, I pray you.

"And the chief butler told his dream to Joseph, and said to him, In my dream, behold, a vine was before me;

"And in the vine were three branches: and it was as though it budded, and her blossoms shot forth; and the clusters thereof brought forth ripe grapes:

"And Pharaoh's cup was in my hand: and I took the grapes, and pressed them into Pharaoh's cup, and I gave the cup into Pharaoh's hand.

"And Joseph said unto him, This is the interpretation of it: The three branches are three days:

"Yet within three days shall Pharaoh lift up your head, and restore you unto your place: and you shall deliver Pharaoh's cup into his hand, after the former manner when you were his butler.

"But think on me when it shall be well with you, and show kindness, I pray you, unto me, and make mention of me unto Pharaoh, and bring me out of this house:

"For indeed I was stolen away out of the land of the Hebrews: and here also have I done nothing that they should put me into the dungeon" (Gen. 40:7-15).

THE WORD OF THE LORD

By this time, Joseph enjoyed comparative freedom from corporeal restraint in the prison. But yet, he was still a prisoner held in this dungeon.

Verses 9 through 19 tell of the dreams of the chief butler and the chief baker. They also tell of Joseph's interpretation of these dreams. In these interpretations, he preached faithfully the Word of the Lord, whether announcing grace or wrath — and so did the Lord Jesus Christ.

Verses 14 and 15 record the fact that Joseph never accused his brothers. He merely said, *"I was stolen away out of the land of the Hebrews."* Likewise, Jesus did not come to condemn but to save.

After hearing the dream, Joseph predicted that in three days, the butler would be restored to his place and position in the palace. Joseph then asked the butler to remember him and make mention of him unto Pharaoh when he was free so that he might be delivered out of this prison. He was required to endure this terrible time within his life, which, incidentally, was laid on him by divine providence. He would do it with meekness and resignation. At the same time, he was under no obligation to stay a moment longer in prison than he could justly help. Rather, he was bound to use all legitimate means to ensure his deliverance, which he did; however, the Lord would not use the butler to effect Joseph's release. He had something far greater in mind than Joseph resuming his place as a slave.

SEVERE STRAITS?

Sometimes, through no fault of our own and sometimes through fault of our own, we are placed by the Lord in severe straits, even as Joseph. Please understand, even as we have already said several times, the Lord is always in charge of all things. His power is so great that even as it regards knowledge of a little sparrow falling to the ground, it does not escape His attention. As well, such detail is exacted that *"the very hairs of our head are all numbered"* (Mat. 10:29-30).

It is impossible for mere mortals to grasp the significance of these statements given by Christ during His earthly sojourn. However, it does give us an idea as to the magnificence of God Almighty, and especially His care for His children.

The Lord allowed Joseph to be put in prison. As well, He had him stay there for a particular period of time, all for a distinct purpose.

As Joseph, in times of difficulty and problems, we should earnestly seek the face of the Lord as to deliverance from these problems. That is not improper. At the same time, we must understand that whatever situation in which we find ourselves, the heavenly Father has desired that we be there, and for excellent reasons. Consequently, we must seek to learn the lesson that He is trying to teach us.

WHAT DID JOSEPH LEARN?

The Scripture tells us, *"The trying of your faith works patience"* (James 1:3). To be sure, Joseph's faith was severely tested, but it was in order to perfect patience.

As well, it was to teach him the same lesson that the Lord would teach the Apostle Paul some 1,700 years in the future. I speak of the grace of God. The Master told the great apostle, *"My grace is sufficient for you: for My strength is made perfect in weakness"* (II Cor. 12:9).

The development of the child of God, whomever that person might be, even Joseph or Paul, is brought about in ways totally contrary to the world.

Whenever the individual comes to Christ, that person is baptized into the death of Christ, buried with Him by baptism into death, and then raised with Him in newness of life (Rom. 6:3-5). Please understand that this is not speaking at all of water baptism, but rather the crucifixion of Christ, with Christ serving as our substitute, so to speak. Our faith literally places us in Christ, which refers to His death, burial, and resurrection. By the means of faith, we came into Christ, and by that means, we remain in Christ.

DEAD TO THE SIN NATURE

As would be obvious, spiritually speaking, whenever you came to Christ, due to the Cross and your faith in that finished work, you literally died to what you were before being *"born again"* (Jn. 3:3).

Paul said: *"Knowing this, that our old man is crucified with Him, that the body of sin might be destroyed* (made ineffective)*, that henceforth we should not serve sin* (the sin nature).

He then said: *"For he who is dead* (dead to the old life) *is freed from sin* (freed from the dominion of the sin nature)*" (Rom. 6:6-7).*

As just stated, all of this means that we are now dead to the sin nature that once ruled us; however, the Scripture doesn't say that the sin nature is dead, but that we are dead rather to the sin nature.

Listen again to Paul: *"Likewise reckon* (account) *you also yourselves to be dead indeed unto sin* (the sin nature)*, but alive unto God through Jesus Christ our Lord"* (Rom. 6:11).

OUR FAITH

If we function as we should function, which refers to our faith being maintained in Christ and the Cross, we will remain dead to the sin nature, and it will have no control over us whatsoever. However, if we shift our faith to other things, irrespective as to what those other things might be, we limit the Holy Spirit as to what He can do within our lives, which guarantees failure. For the Holy Spirit to work as only He can work, for He is God, our faith must be maintained in the finished work of Christ (Rom. 8:1-2).

The problem is that we have a tendency to allow our faith to drift to other things, and when this happens, the *"old man"* suddenly comes alive again, and we find ourselves in trouble. In fact, this particular fight of faith, as previously stated, is a constant struggle (I Tim. 6:12).

Concerning this, the great apostle also said: *"For the flesh* (self-efforts) *lusts against the Spirit* (Holy Spirit)*, and the Spirit against the flesh: and these are contrary the one to the other: so that you cannot do the things that you would"* (Gal. 5:17).

The flesh pertains to our own self-efforts and our own ability and strength, which, incidentally, the Lord cannot use. Everything He does must be done by and through the power of the Holy Spirit. To subdue the flesh, the following must be done.

SUBDUING THE FLESH

As stated, the flesh, as Paul used the word, pertains to our own ability, motivation, education, talents, strength, etc. In other words, it speaks of our trying to perfect holiness and righteousness by our own religious efforts rather than the prescribed order that the Lord has given unto us, which is the Cross of Christ. If the believer doesn't understand the Cross— and I speak of how the Cross effects our sanctification—then without fail, the believer is going to attempt to subdue the flesh by his own machinations, ability, and strength. He will never succeed but, in fact, will only make the flesh and, thereby, failure more predominant.

The flesh is subdued only by the believer understanding that everything he needs comes to him through what Jesus did at the Cross, and that he will receive nothing from God but that it come through the finished work of Christ. It is absolutely imperative that the believer understands this. We have what we have from the Lord not because of our denominations with which we are associated, our churches (as important as that may be), our good works, etc., but by and through what Jesus did at the Cross. Whenever the believer anchors his faith in the Cross, the flesh will automatically be subdued. In fact, this is the only way it can be subdued. Then we are in Christ, and Christ is in us (Jn. 14:20). The *"in Christ"* position is the only place for the child of God. We arrive there by our faith being in Christ and what He did for us at the Cross, and it is maintained in the same manner.

DIFFICULTIES

However, for the believer to come to this place and to remain in this place, oftentimes, the Lord must bring the believer through difficulties that force him to depend exclusively on Christ and not at all on himself. The Lord will often put us in a position to where our own strength and ability are woefully insufficient. In other words, we have to trust Him, have to believe Him, and have to look to Him.

Joseph was in that type of situation: unless the Lord brought him out of that prison, there was no way that he could be released. So, Joseph could grow bitter and blame God and other people, or he could allow the Holy Spirit to mold him, make him, and humble him — which he did, and which the Lord intended. Millions of Christians have tried to circumvent the *prison experience*, but to no avail. Sooner or later in one way or the other, the Lord puts us in a difficult situation.

It is all for purpose and is intended to cut away the dead branches in order that we may look more and more to the True Vine that we might bring forth much fruit (Jn., Chpt. 15).

THE CHIEF BAKER

"When the chief baker saw that the interpretation was good, he said unto Joseph, I also was in my dream, and, behold, I had three white baskets on my head:

"And in the uppermost basket there was of all manner of bakemeats for Pharaoh; and the birds did eat them out of the basket upon my head" (Gen. 40:16-17).

God alone knows the future, and He is able to reveal it to men, should He so desire.

The manner in which the Holy Spirit used Joseph in this instance would come under the heading of three modern gifts of the Spirit: discerning of spirits, the word of knowledge, and the word of wisdom (I Cor. 12:8-10).

As we shall see, even though the butler forgot Joseph, which was the will of God, he would remember him some two years later when it was God's time for him to be released. Waiting is a part of faith.

One thing is certain: the chief butler didn't have long to wait to see if Joseph's interpretation was correct — only three days.

Evidently, the chief baker had not been too anxious to relate his dream to Joseph, probably thinking that such was a waste of time. However, upon hearing the interpretation given to the chief butler, and knowing that in three days Joseph's accuracy would be proven, he ventured forth to relate his dream.

THREE DAYS

"And Joseph answered and said, This is the interpretation thereof: The three baskets are three days:

"Yet within three days shall Pharaoh lift up your head from off you, and shall hang you on a tree; and the birds shall eat your flesh from off you.

"And it came to pass the third day, which was Pharaoh's birthday, that he made a feast unto all his servants: and he lifted up the head of the chief butler and of the chief baker among his servants.

"And he restored the chief butler unto his butlership again; and he gave the cup into Pharaoh's hand:

"But he hanged the chief baker: as Joseph had interpreted to them.

"Yet did not the chief butler remember Joseph, but forgot him" (Gen. 40:18-23).

I can well surmise that the chief baker was not at all pleased with Joseph's interpretation and probably laughed it off. Nevertheless, in three days, a great feast was conducted by Pharaoh, celebrating his birthday, and both the chief butler and the chief baker were released from prison. Thus far, it was exactly as Joseph had predicted.

A FULFILLMENT OF THE PREDICTION

At a given point in time, the narrative seems to indicate that Pharaoh suddenly announced that the chief butler was restored to his former position, but that the chief baker was to hang, which he did. So, in the exact manner that Joseph predicted, in that exact manner was it carried out.

But yet, the chief butler forgot Joseph, which seems to indicate that it was the will of God that this be done. It is certain that if the Lord had intended for Joseph to be released at that time, He would have pressed hard upon the mind of the chief butler. That not being the case, we must come to the conclusion that the Lord had other purposes in mind, which become very obvious in the next chapter. While Joseph may have been forgotten by man, he definitely was not forgotten by God.

As well, one might very well note that if Joseph had been released at this time, he would have been just another slave. However, the way the Lord did this thing, even though it was hard on Joseph's flesh to stay two more years in this dungeon, still, it would all prove to be the best thing.

"Sinners Jesus will receive
"Sound this word of grace to all
"Who the heavenly pathway leave,
"All who linger, all who fall."

"Come, and He will give you rest;
"Trust Him, for His Word is plain;
"He will take the sinfulest;
"Christ receives sinful men."

"Now my heart condemns me not,
"Pure before the law I stand;
"He who cleansed me from all spot,
"Satisfied its last demand."

"Christ receives sinful men,
"Even me with all my sin;
"Purged from every spot and stain,
"Heaven with Him I enter in."

JOSEPH

CHAPTER

6

THE DREAM

CHAPTER SIX

THE DREAM

"And it came to pass at the end of two full years, that Pharaoh dreamed: and, behold, he stood by the river" (Gen. 41:1).

This is two years after Joseph had given the interpretation to the butler and the baker.

To be sure, this was another test for Joseph, and a difficult test at that. It was the *"test of delay,"* but God's delays are not cruel. They all have a purpose (Horton).

Again, the Lord used a dream in order to bring about several things. The dream would bring about the release of Joseph. More importantly, while addressing itself to the present, it would more particularly address itself to the distant future, in fact, a time which has not even yet come to pass. Momentarily we will go into detail as it regards this prediction of futuristic events. In fact, it pertains to the great outpouring of the Holy Spirit in the last days and, as well, the coming time of great trouble called the great tribulation period as it regards Israel (Mat. 24:21).

In the dream, Pharaoh stood by the river, which, incidentally, was the Nile.

The Egyptians believed the Nile to be the giver of life. Consequently, by the Lord giving this man such a dream and having him in the dream to stand by the Nile is at least a great part of the reason that Pharaoh placed such stock in these dreams. Otherwise, he might have passed it off as incidental.

THE DREAM AS IT WAS GIVEN

"And, behold, there came up out of the river seven well favored cattle and fatfleshed; and they fed in a meadow.

"And, behold, seven other cattle came up after them out of the river, ill favored and leanfleshed; and stood by the other cattle upon the brink of the river.

"And the ill favored and leanfleshed cattle did eat up the seven well favored and fat cattle. So Pharaoh awoke.

"And he slept and dreamed the second time: and, behold, seven ears of corn came up upon one stalk, rank and good.

"And, behold, seven thin ears and blasted with the east wind sprung up after them.

"And the seven thin ears devoured the seven rank and full ears. And Pharaoh awoke, and, behold, it was a dream" (Gen. 41:2-7).

According to some of the sages of old, the heifer was regarded by the ancient Egyptians as a symbol of the earth, agriculture, and the nourishment derived therefrom. It was therefore natural that the succession of seven prosperous years should be represented by seven thriving cows.

That they were coming up out of the Nile was the same thing as God speaking to Pharaoh, at least in his heathen thinking.

THE LORD GAVE THE DREAMS

We find that the dream of Pharaoh was doubled by the Lord, for of a certainty it was the Lord who gave the monarch these two dreams.

Both dreams were simple to Pharaoh, but yet, he lacked understanding. Seven fat cows came up out of the river, and they began to feed or graze in a meadow.

However, then we had seven other cattle coming up out of the river, but rather lean and undernourished. These which were undernourished came up to the fat cattle and ate them up.

Pharaoh awoke and then went back to sleep that same night, or else, it speaks of the next night. The dream was basically the same as the first one, but different ingredients were used.

The second dream portrayed a stalk coming up containing seven sheaves of grain, fat and healthy. Then another stalk came out of the ground with seven thin sheaves, which then devoured the seven healthy sheaves.

As we shall see, in this simple dream given to this heathen monarch, the future would be foretold concerning times soon to come and, as well, happenings into the distant future that have not even yet come to pass.

THE MAGICIANS OF EGYPT

"And it came to pass in the morning that his spirit was troubled; and he sent and called for all the magicians of Egypt, and all the wise men thereof: and Pharaoh told them his dream; but there was none who could interpret them unto Pharaoh" (Gen. 41:8).

Pharaoh dreamed of seven cattle and seven ears of corn. The Egyptian *Book of the Dead,* now in the British Museum in London, with its sacred cows and mystic number seven — a book beyond doubt well known to Pharaoh — must have helped to convince the king that this double dream was supernatural.

Considering that the Lord used the Nile River, cows, and stalks of grain out of the earth as symbols in this dream, such made it very important to Pharaoh, who considered these things to be gods in their own right. Since the dream was doubled, and more than likely given in one night, the monarch was most desirous of learning the meaning of what he had dreamed.

THE WISE MEN

The magicians of Egypt, along with the wise men, were the most learned and knowledgeable of their kind in the world of that day. Concerning these individuals, history says that they claimed mysterious knowledge of magic, divination, and astrology. They knew all the ancient magical inscriptions and were skilled in deciphering and interpreting them.

That they could not explain the dreams, though couched in the symbolic language of the time, was, no doubt, surprising; but *"the things of God knows no man, but the Spirit of God"* (I Cor. 2:11), and they to whom the Spirit does reveal them (I Cor. 2:10).

It is no different presently. The only people in the world who have a blueprint for the future are the people of God who know their Bibles. It is the Bible alone that tells us what the future holds regarding the nations of this world. And yet, despite the fact of such startling information, precious few take the time to peruse the contents of the Word of God.

THE FUTURE

Concerning the future, in brief, the Bible teaches that the Rapture of the church could take place at any moment (I Thess. 4:13-18). This will be followed at some point by seven years of great tribulation, which, believe it or not, Pharaoh saw in his dreams (II Thess. 2:7-8). In fact, these seven years of great tribulation will begin at the moment the Antichrist signs the seven-year agreement with Israel and other countries, guaranteeing the borders of Israel, etc. As stated, at that moment, this seven-year period begins.

The great tribulation period, lasting some seven years, will be concluded by the battle of Armageddon, which will bring about the second coming of the Lord. That will be the most cataclysmic event that the world will have ever seen. It will be the fulfillment of Daniel's interpretation of the dream of Nebuchadnezzar.

The great prophet-statesman said: *"Forasmuch as you saw that the stone was cut out of the mountain without hands, and that it broke in pieces the iron, the brass, the clay, the silver, and the gold, the great God has made known to the king what shall come to pass hereafter: and the dream is certain, and the interpretation thereof sure"* (Dan. 2:45).

That *stone* is Christ. At the second coming, He will smash in pieces all of the governments of men and, thereby, take control of the entirety of the world Himself. Isaiah said of Him: *"And the government shall be upon His shoulder: and His name shall be called Wonderful, Counselor, the Mighty God, the Everlasting Father, the Prince of Peace."*

He then said, *"Of the increase of His government and peace there shall be no end, upon the throne of David, and upon His kingdom, to order it, and to establish it with judgment and with justice from henceforth even forever. The zeal of the Lord of Hosts will perform this"* (Isa. 9:6-7).

PROPHECY

Under Christ, the world will then enter into 1,000 years of peace, with Satan locked away in the bottomless pit, along with all of his fallen angels and demon spirits. At the end of that thousand-year period, he will be loosed for a little season but will be put down quickly. The world will then be renovated by fire, and the New Jerusalem will come down from God out of Heaven to rest upon this earth. Then God will literally change His headquarters from Heaven to earth (Rev., Chpts. 20-22).

In fact, about one-third of the Bible is prophecy, with another third being instruction, and the remaining third being history. No other book in the world even remotely compares with the Word of God because it is the Word of God. This means that it does not merely contain the Word of God but, in fact, is the Word of God.

Without God and His Word, all the magicians and wise men of the world have no clue as to what the future holds. However, as stated, the Bible portrays that future to us. Man would do well to heed its contents! The wise men of Pharaoh's day could not interpret the dreams or the times. Joseph could because the Lord revealed it to him. It did not mean that Joseph was more intelligent or brilliant than these so-called wise men, but that the Lord gave him the interpretation to all these dreams.

The dreams that will be interpreted will, in a sense, be the very first glimpse into the future regarding nations, unless we would count that given by Enoch. This actually wasn't given to us in the Old Testament, but was recorded only in brief in the New (Jude, Vs. 14).

JOSEPH

"Then spoke the chief butler unto Pharaoh, saying, I do remember my faults this day:

"Pharaoh was angry with his servants, and put me in ward in the captain of the guard's house, both me and the chief baker:

"*And we dreamed a dream in one night, I and he; we dreamed each man according to the interpretation of his dream.*

"*And there was there with us a young man, an Hebrew, servant to the captain of the guard; and we told him, and he interpreted to us our dreams; to each man according to his dream he did interpret.*

"*And it came to pass, as he interpreted to us, so it was; me he restored unto my office, and him he hanged*" (Gen. 41:9-13).

The great court of Pharaoh, the mightiest monarch on the face of the earth, had come to its proverbial wit's end, which means that no one had the answer. The chief butler suddenly spoke up concerning Joseph and his experience regarding the interpretation of his dream, as well as the dream of the chief baker, when they both were in prison.

THE HAND OF GOD

The pronouns (he) in the latter part of Verse 13 refer to Pharaoh and not Joseph. While Joseph interpreted the dreams, it was Pharaoh who restored the man to his office and hanged the other one.

As we observe the entirety of the scene unfolding before us, we see the hand of God in all things. The Lord was getting the earth ready for a great harvest, which would be followed by famine. At the appropriate time, He would give dreams to Pharaoh. They were dreams, incidentally, which the mighty monarch could not interpret, nor could anyone in his kingdom, at least as far as his wise men were concerned. The Lord then caused the chief butler to vividly remember the incident with Joseph concerning his dreams of some two years before.

As well, during these two years, the Lord was further educating Joseph in His ways. The Scripture is not exactly clear as to how long Joseph actually stayed in prison. The two years mentioned only concern the time from Joseph's interpretation of the dreams, regarding the butler and the baker, to the time he was released from prison. How long he spent in prison altogether, we aren't told. Many think it was approximately seven years, which could well have been the case.

JOSEPH AND PHARAOH

"Then Pharaoh sent and called Joseph, and they brought him hastily out of the dungeon: and he shaved himself, and changed his raiment, and came in unto Pharaoh" (Gen. 41:14).

During all of this previous time of preparation (and preparation it was), had Joseph become bitter, hateful, and haughty, and had he held grudges against his brothers or blamed God—he would never have come to this place to which the Lord would elevate him. This should be a great lesson for all of us.

As I've previously stated, everything, as it regards the child of God, presents itself as a test. How do we act? How do we react?

The believer is to do everything according to the Word of God irrespective as to what my brother might do to me or how bad it might be. I must not grow bitter in my heart toward him. I must pray for him because that's exactly what Christ told us to do. He said, *"Love your enemies, bless them who curse you, do good to them who hate you, and pray for them which despitefully use you, and persecute you"* (Mat. 5:44).

OBEYING CHRIST

This doesn't mean to condone their actions, nor does it mean to have fellowship with them. In fact, unless they repent, fellowship is impossible. However, none of that precludes the command of Christ that we love them, bless them, do good to them, and pray for them.

Let the reader understand the following: while following the admonition of Christ will definitely bless the individual in question, it is actually done more so for the one who has been wronged than anyone else. Obeying Christ will stop bitterness, ill-will, rancor, and anger.

Whenever we harbor ill-will against someone, thereby, refusing to forgive him, in a sense, that person owns us. Let me explain that:

We think about them constantly, as to how we can get even with them, what we can do to them, etc. As stated, they own our thoughts, in effect, owning us.

Whenever we properly forgive someone, even as Joseph forgave his brothers, we then release them to the Lord, letting Him take care of the situation.

However, we should remember this as well: as stated, forgiveness doesn't mean that fellowship can be restored. As we shall see, when the time came when Joseph's brothers came before him, he did not immediately reveal himself to them. In fact, he tested them thoroughly to see if they were the same men who sold him into Egyptian bondage, or whether they had changed. We are obligated to do the same as well!

THE WORDS OF PHARAOH

"And Pharaoh said unto Joseph, I have dreamed a dream, and there is none who can interpret it: and I have heard say of you, that you can understand a dream to interpret it" (Gen. 41:15).

The evidence is that Joseph, after shaving and changing his clothes, came immediately from the dungeon to the palace. I wonder what his thoughts were as he walked into one of the most palatial settings in the entirety of the world. Had the Lord given him any clue at all as to what was about to happen?

This one thing is certain: any believer who is truly right with God is master of the situation, irrespective as to the setting or how powerful the unsaved individuals present might be.

Any saved individual is a child of God. As such, there is an authority that accompanies the position. Despite this being the palace of the mightiest monarch on the face of the earth, Joseph was supreme. He alone held the answer to the dilemma at hand. So, during one of the few times in history, the powers that be would consult with a man of God. He would not be sorry!

GIVE THE GLORY TO GOD

"And Joseph answered Pharaoh, saying, It is not in me: God shall give Pharaoh an answer of peace" (Gen. 41:16).

Joseph was quick to give the glory to God. He took no credit for what was about to transpire, even as he shouldn't have taken any credit. This is very, very important.

It is hard for God to bless many people for the simple reason that they tend to think that they have made some contribution to the effort. None of us has. Anything and everything that is spiritual always comes totally and completely from the Lord. We are merely an instrument at best and must always understand that.

Pharaoh, knowing little or nothing about Jehovah, gave Joseph the credit for these things he had heard concerning the interpretation of dreams, and especially the fact that what had been predicted came to pass exactly as predicted. Knowing that Pharaoh understood nothing about Jehovah, Joseph could have easily overlooked this part. However, he was quick to correct the monarch, saying, *"It is not in me,"* with him then telling Pharaoh that if the answer came, it would be God who did it.

THE DREAMS RELATED

*"And Pharaoh said unto Joseph, In my dream, behold, I
stood upon the bank of the river:*

*"And, behold, there came up out of the river seven cattle,
fatfleshed and well favored; and they fed in a meadow:*

*"And, behold, seven other cattle came up after them,
poor and very ill favored and leanfleshed, such as I never
saw in all the land of Egypt for badness:*

*"And the lean and the ill favored cattle did eat up the
first seven fat cattle:*

*"And when they had eaten them up, it could not be
known that they had eaten them; but they were still ill
favored, as at the beginning. So I awoke.*

*"And I saw in my dream, and, behold, seven ears came
up in one stalk, full and good:*

*"And, behold, seven ears, withered, thin, and blasted
with the east wind, sprung up after them:*

*"And the thin ears devoured the seven good ears: and I
told this unto the magicians; but there was none who could
declare it to me"* (Gen. 41:17-24).

The dreams had made such an impression upon Pharaoh
that he felt he had to have an answer to their meaning. This
was not a case of mere curiosity, but rather a compulsion
actually placed in the heart of the monarch by the Lord. It
is ironic: Pharaoh was looked at by the Egyptians as a *"god"*
in any case, but yet, the interpretation of a dream completely
disproved this fallacy.

That which seemed to be more confusing to the monarch was the fact that the lean cattle ate up the fat cattle but showed no improvement. It was the same with the seven stalks of grain. The thin sheaves devoured the seven good sheaves but were none the better. The monarch then emphatically stated to Joseph concerning the interpretation of all of this, *"There was none who could declare it to me."*

WHAT GOD IS ABOUT TO DO

"And Joseph said unto Pharaoh, The dream of Pharaoh is one: God has shown Pharaoh what He is about to do" (Gen. 41:25).

Discoveries about 100 years ago at the First Cataract and at El-Kab record the fact of this seven years of famine. The date is given as 1700 B.C. This date accords with accepted Bible chronology.

As Joseph says in Verse 32, the dream, although one, was doubled in order to denote its divine certainty and, as well, to portray its immediate happening and its futuristic happening.

For those whom God would use, in some way, there must be a prison before there can be a palace. The problem of self demands it.

This one statement in Verse 25, as given by Joseph, proclaims the fact that God is over all. He controls the weather, He controls nations, and He controls men. By that, I do not mean to say, nor does the Scripture teach, that everything is predestined; however, the idea is, God is in charge and not man. It's hard for man to understand that or even to agree to that.

Even though this one dream that came in two parts had a double fulfillment, Pharaoh, of course, would be interested in that which was coming in the immediate future, hence, Joseph saying, *"God has shown Pharaoh what He is about to do."*

THE INTERPRETATION

"The seven good cattle are seven years; and the seven good ears are seven years: the dream is one.

"And the seven thin and ill favored cattle that came up after them are seven years; and the seven empty ears blasted with the east wind shall be seven years of famine.

"This is the thing which I have spoken unto Pharaoh: What God is about to do He shows unto Pharaoh.

"Behold, there come seven years of great plenty through-out all the land of Egypt:

"And there shall arise after them seven years of famine; and all the plenty shall be forgotten in the land of Egypt; and the famine shall consume the land;

"And the plenty shall not be known in the land by reason of that famine following; for it shall be very grievous.

"And for that the dream was doubled unto Pharaoh twice; it is because the thing is established by God, and God will shortly bring it to pass" (Gen. 41:26-32).

Exactly as to how the Lord moved upon Joseph as it regarded this interpretation, we aren't told. More than likely,

He revealed it to his spirit and did it in such a way that Joseph knew beyond the shadow of a doubt that what he was saying was correct. As well, it was so right that Pharaoh accepted the interpretation immediately. In other words, Pharaoh felt in his spirit that this was the right interpretation also.

The seven fat cattle represented seven years of tremendous harvest that would come to Egypt, generating perhaps the greatest abundance the nation had ever known. This would begin immediately, possibly with the coming planting season.

Then immediately following the seven years of plenty would come seven years of famine, which would devour the entire surplus of the seven years of plenty, and would do so to such an extent that it would leave nothing. The Scripture says, *"the famine shall consume the land"* (Vs. 30).

THE PROPHETIC ANALYSIS

The interpretation as given by Joseph, which greatly concerned Pharaoh, was to take place in the immediate future. However, due to the fact of the dream being double, it has an end-time meaning, as well, which will be of far greater magnitude than that which would take place in the near future.

It is as follows: We know that this terrible famine which would follow the seven years of plenty would ultimately bring Joseph's brothers to him, along with his father Jacob. In a sense, this represents Israel coming to Christ, which they shall do at the conclusion of the seven-year great tribulation period. This will be at the second coming of the Lord. So, the seven years of famine point to the coming seven-year great tribulation period prophesied by Daniel and foretold by Jesus (Dan. 9:27; Mat. 24:21).

THE EAST WIND

As well, the east wind mentioned in Verse 27 localizes the great tribulation period that is coming, which will affect the entire earth but will have its beginnings in the Middle East.

As it regards the seven years of plenty that immediately preceded the seven years of famine, by looking at it in the prophetic sense, I believe we should take the number *seven* in the following manner: As is known, the number seven is God's number of perfection. At any rate, I believe the Lord has told me that before the seven years of great tribulation come upon this earth, there is going to be a harvest of souls such as the world or the church has never seen. As stated, I believe the Lord has told me this. It will be the last worldwide move before the coming great tribulation. Due to the advancement of modern technology, millions of souls can easily be brought to Christ as the Holy Spirit moves in all of His convicting power, etc.

Furthermore, I believe this ministry (Jimmy Swaggart Ministries) is going to play a part in this great harvest. In fact, as I dictate these notes in April 2013, I believe we are even now in the preparatory stages.

Regarding the church, the Bible tells us that the following will take place: Paul said that some will *"depart from the faith, giv-*

ing heed to seducing spirits, and doctrines of devils (demons)" (I Tim. 4:1). So, in essence, we have two things taking place: a tremendous harvest of souls and, at the same time, a great departure from the faith. Regrettably, the latter has already begun.

THE CROSS

The dividing line between the true church and the apostate church will be and, in fact, is the Cross of Christ. Actually, the Cross has always been the dividing line, but it will be and is now more pronounced than ever. In other words, faith is either going to have to be placed in Jesus Christ and Him crucified or else in other things. To place one's faith in something else means simply that *"Christ shall profit you nothing" (Gal. 5:2)*. That means that all of this will end exactly as it began.

From the beginning (we go to Chapter 4 of Genesis), we find Abel offering up the sacrifice of an innocent victim, a lamb, and Cain offering up the work and labor of his own hands in sacrifice, which God would not accept. While both were sacrifices, only one was acceptable to God because it spoke of man's sin and man's redemption, which would be gained through the sacrificial offering of Christ Himself. In effect, Cain's sacrifice stated that he wasn't a sinner and, thereby, didn't need a Redeemer. He was willing to acknowledge God by offering up the sacrifice as he did, but not willing to admit what he was and what he needed. It is the same presently! It is the Cross or nothing, as it has always been the Cross or nothing!

"Blessed be the fountain of blood,
"To a world of sinners revealed;
"Blessed be the dear Son of God;
"Only by His stripes we are healed."

"Tho' I've wandered far from His fold,
"Bringing to my heart pain and woe,
"Wash me in the blood of the Lamb,
"And I shall be whiter than snow."

"Thorny was the crown that He wore,
"And the Cross His body overcame;
"Grievous were the sorrows He bore,
"But He suffered thus not in vain."

"May I to that fountain be led,
"Made to cleanse my sins here below;
"Wash me in the blood that He shed,
"And I shall be whiter than snow."

"Father, I have wandered from Thee,
"Often has my heart gone astray;
"Crimson do my sins seem to me
"Water cannot wash them away."

"Jesus to that fountain of Thine,
"Leaning on Your promise I go;
"Cleanse me by Your washing divine,
"And I shall be whiter than snow."

JOSEPH

JOSEPH, VICEROY OF EGYPT

JOSEPH, VICEROY OF EGYPT

"Now therefore let Pharaoh look out a man discreet and wise, and set him over the land of Egypt.

"Let Pharaoh do this, and let him appoint officers over the land, and take up the fifth part of the land of Egypt in the seven plentiful years.

"And let them gather all the food of those good years that come, and lay up corn under the hand of Pharaoh, and let them keep food in the cities.

"And that food shall be for store to the land against the seven years of famine, which shall be in the land of Egypt; that the land perish not through the famine" (Gen. 41:33-36).

Joseph was made the lord of Egypt, even as Christ was made the Lord of the Gentiles.

This famine was designed by God not only to bless and instruct Egypt, but mainly to be the means of bringing Joseph's brothers in repentance to his feet. As well, it is all a picture of present and future facts.

The true Joseph in his present rejection by his brethren, and we speak of the Lord Jesus Christ, takes to Himself an election from among the Gentiles. The completion of that election, if this portrayal may be so interpreted, will be followed by *"the time of Jacob's trouble."* The effect of this trouble will be to cause the sons of Israel to recognize Him whom they have pierced and to mourn and weep (Zech. 12:11-14).

THE WORD OF THE LORD

Joseph's suggestion to Pharaoh for addressing this coming situation, without a doubt, was given to him by the Lord as well. As stated, it seems the interpretation so satisfied the monarch that he never doubted the words of Joseph. Of course, the Lord had prepared everything for this moment. This one thing is certain: Despite the fact that Joseph had been in prison for several years, not one person stepped up to accuse him at this particular time. This proves beyond the shadow of a doubt the absolute falseness of the charges that had placed him in prison to begin with.

I wonder how Joseph felt when Pharaoh sent for him. He had languished in prison for several years, and now he would go stand before Pharaoh. Regarding those who were sent by Pharaoh to retrieve Joseph, did they give him any hint as to why he was being called before the mightiest monarch at that time on the face of the earth?

Whatever the situation may have been, it is absolutely certain that the Lord had prepared him minutely for this moment. In fact, he would not only go from the prison to the palace but, as well, to the place and position of being the second most powerful man in Egypt and, more than likely, the world as well.

JOSEPH CHOSEN

"And the thing was good in the eyes of Pharaoh, and in the eyes of all his servants.

"And Pharaoh said unto his servants, Can we find such a one as this is, a man in whom the Spirit of God is?

"And Pharaoh said unto Joseph, Forasmuch as God has shown you all this, there is none so discreet and wise as you are:

"You shall be over my house, and according unto your word shall all my people be ruled: only in the throne will I be greater than you.

"And Pharaoh said unto Joseph, See, I have set you over all the land of Egypt.

"And Pharaoh took off his ring from his hand, and put it upon Joseph's hand, and arrayed him in vestures of fine linen, and put a gold chain about his neck;

"And he made him to ride in the second chariot which he had; and they cried before him, Bow the knee: and he made him ruler over all the land of Egypt.

"And Pharaoh said unto Joseph, I am Pharaoh, and without you shall no man lift up his hand or foot in all the land of Egypt.

"And Pharaoh called Joseph's name Zaphnath-paa-neah; and he gave him to wife Asenath the daughter of Poti-pherah priest of On. And Joseph went out over all the land of Egypt" (Gen. 41:37-45).

After Joseph suggested to Pharaoh what should be done, the monarch instantly suggested that Joseph be made the prime minister, or as the Bible uses the term, the governor. He used a term that is familiar to us but needs explanation. He said, *"a man in whom the Spirit of God is."*

THE SPIRIT OF GOD?

The Hebrew would have been *"Ruach-Elohim"* and would have been understood by Pharaoh as referring to the sagacity and intelligence of a deity. Other than that, he would have had no knowledge as to what or who the Spirit of God actually was, and his understanding would have been far different than the understanding of Joseph.

So, in a moment's time, Joseph was promoted to the august position of the governor of all of Egypt, and was thus one of the most powerful men in the world.

Pharaoh made him greater than anyone else in Egypt except himself, and made his authority to cover the entirety of the land of Egypt. Furthermore, he took off his ring from his hand *"and put it upon Joseph's hand,"* which proclaimed the fact that his position was real and not merely honorary. The vestures of fine linen made Joseph a part of the priestly class. The gold chain about his neck pertained to that which was worn by persons of distinction. Joseph's authority was to be absolute and universal, which it was. There was no part of Egypt over which he didn't have control.

The very name that Pharaoh gave Joseph, *Zaphnath-paaneah*, was prophetic. As his Hebrew name, Joseph means *"Jehovah shall add"*; his Egyptian name means *"life more abundant."* So, in essence, both of his names meant *"Jehovah shall add life more abundant,"* which portrays Christ as well.

Jesus said, *"I am come that they might have life, and that they might have it more abundantly"* (Jn. 10:10).

THIRTY YEARS OLD

"And Joseph was thirty years old when he stood before Pharaoh king of Egypt. And Joseph went out from the presence of Pharaoh, and went throughout all the land of Egypt" (Gen. 41:46).

Joseph was 30 years old when he stood before Pharaoh, and Jesus was 30 years old when He began His public ministry.

Concerning the seven years of plenty, Joseph's predictions proved to be exact.

The harvests were greater than Egypt had ever experienced, so great, in fact, that it could not be counted or measured.

It was not without meaning that the Holy Spirit through Moses told us that Joseph was 30 years old when he stood before Pharaoh. As we have just stated, Joseph — as a type of Christ — began his public ministry, so to speak, at the same age that the greater Joseph would begin His public ministry.

Christ was 30 years old when He came forth to minister to the people (Lk. 3:23).

As Joseph *"went throughout all the land of Egypt"* as it refers to his authority in carrying out the commands of Pharaoh, likewise, the Lord Jesus Christ, rejected by His brethren, has gone out over the entirety of the Gentile world in order to gather the grain of souls.

SEVEN YEARS OF PLENTY

"And in the seven plenteous years the earth brought forth by handfuls.

"And he gathered up all the food of the seven years, which were in the land of Egypt, and laid up the food in the cities: the food of the field, which was round about every city, laid he up in the same.

"And Joseph gathered corn (grain) *as the sand of the sea, very much, until he left numbering; for it was without number"* (Gen. 41:47-49).

Exactly as Joseph predicted is exactly as it happened. There were seven years of harvests as Egypt had never known. In fact, it was so great that the Scripture says they quit trying to number or count the bushels. No doubt, the Lord gave Joseph great wisdom during all of this time in that the decisions he made were not ideas out of his own mind, but that which was given to him by the Lord. The Lord would not have given him this position without preparing him and guiding him in this position.

As we've already stated, the latter part of the dream, which spoke of the seven ears of grain that were fat and healthy, and then the seven ears of grain that were blasted and withered, are yet to be fulfilled. As it took the famine to bring Jacob to Joseph, it will take the great tribulation to bring Jacob to Jesus.

However, at the same time, if the seven ears of grain that were blasted and withered speak of the great tribulation that will last for seven years, then the seven ears of grain that are fat and healthy speak of a harvest of souls such as the world or the church has never seen.

We are living in the closing days of the church age. If the calendars of the past 2,000 years are correct, the church is now 2,014 years old. Every 2,000 years, something tremendously spiritual has taken place:

- From the time of Adam and Eve to the time of Abraham was a time frame of approximately 2,000 years. To Abraham was given the doctrine of justification by faith (Gen. 15:6). It presents itself as a hallmark in time.
- From the time of Abraham to the time of Christ presents itself as another 2,000 years. Of course, while the Law came by Moses, grace and truth came by Jesus Christ. The first advent of Christ presents itself as the greatest moment in human history. There, salvation was effected at the Cross, with Jesus rising from the dead.
- Now, we come to the third 2,000-year time frame that will usher in not only the Rapture of the church, which

could take place at any time, but, as well, the second coming, which will be the most cataclysmic event the world has ever known.

THE RAPTURE OF THE CHURCH

I do not personally believe that the Lord is coming back for a weak, emaciated, barren church. While it is true that the great departure of the faith will take place and has already begun, still, the Lord has a people — individuals scattered all over the world — who truly love Him. This is why the Message of the Cross is so very, very important.

Please note the following:

- We read of the early church in the book of Acts and the Epistles. Led by the Apostle Paul, it touched much of the known world of that day with the Gospel.
- Regrettably, when the apostles died and those who knew them, the church gradually went into spiritual declension, which ultimately brought about the Catholic Church. Thank God for the Reformation, which began in the early 1600s. It changed everything.
- Then the great Holiness Movement began to spring up all over the world, in a sense, bringing the church back to the Cross.
- At approximately the turn of the 20th century, the mighty outpouring of the Holy Spirit (respecting the latter rain) began to take place, which has resulted in

some 500 million people, it is said, being baptized with the Holy Spirit with the evidence of speaking with other tongues (Acts 2:4). True enough, Bible days were here again.

■ Sadly and regrettably, the great Pentecostal move began to wane and weaken, with the church now coming full circle, and the Message of the Cross, exactly as it was given in early church times, being brought to bear by the Holy Spirit. The church began with the Message of the Cross, and it is going to go out, I believe, with the Message of the Cross.

Martin Luther said, *"As one viewed the Cross, so one viewed the Reformation."* We can say the same presently that as one views the Cross, one views the Word of God.

OUTPOURING OF THE HOLY SPIRIT

I believe that in these last days there is going to be a great harvest of souls, and, of course, I refer to people being saved. At the same time, I feel that hundreds of thousands are going to be baptized with the Holy Spirit. I believe the Lord has informed me of this as well.

On a Saturday afternoon a few weeks ago (as I dictate these notes), the Lord began to impress upon me to go to prayer. We have a prayer meeting every Saturday morning at the ministry, which convenes at 10 a.m. I never miss that, but now the Lord was impressing upon me to go again and pray.

Upon going to prayer, the Lord brought back to me a promise that He had made back in the early 1970s. He told me at that time to set aside a particular service in the crusades, which turned out to be Sunday afternoon, for believers to be baptized with the Holy Spirit. He even told me to air these services over television, and we did, which resulted in untold thousands being filled with the Spirit.

At that time, He told me that if I would believe Him, in one of these services He would fill as many as a thousand people with the Holy Spirit. As the months rolled into several years, we saw thousands filled with the Spirit, but never as many as a thousand in a single service.

The year was 1987. We were at Madison Square Garden in New York City. It seats 22,000 people. It was packed to capacity that Sunday afternoon. As usual, I preached on the baptism with the Holy Spirit in that particular service and then called those forward who desired to be filled. They lined up down every aisle all the way to the back of the building and then around the back. The Lord moved in a powerful way.

Almost immediately after the service, Frances and I had to fly to London, England. With London being about six hours ahead of the United States, we arrived there in the afternoon of the next day.

After getting settled in the room, inasmuch as the hotel was immediately beside Hyde Park, I told Frances that I was going over to the park and walk and pray for awhile, which I did.

TEN THOUSAND IN A SINGLE SERVICE

While in prayer that afternoon, the Lord brought the service to mind that we had just concluded at Madison Square Garden, and then He asked me, *"How many were baptized with the Holy Spirit?"*

I thought for just a moment and then, realizing how large that building was, how many people were present, and how many came forward to be baptized with the Holy Spirit, I knew immediately why the Lord had asked me this question. Well over a thousand had been filled with the Spirit in that one service. In fact, people were filled with the Spirit that afternoon who are now pastoring churches in greater New York and elsewhere. I had not even thought about how many were filled, but I instantly knew that the Lord had kept His promise to me.

Then the Lord spoke to my heart, saying, *"If you will believe Me, I will fill as many as 10,000 in a single service."*

After my time of prayer ended, I wondered, *"Did the Lord really say that to me, or did it come out of my mind?"*

At any rate, due to the events that followed, what few times I thought about it, I wondered how in the world could such happen.

At any rate, the Saturday afternoon in the month of March 2013, as I went to prayer, the Lord brought all of this back to me, plus that which He had said to me in Hyde Park in London, England: *"If you believe Me, I will fill as many as 10,000."*

While in prayer those few days ago (March 2013), the Lord quickly brought my mind to television and how it covers untold millions of people. That would make it very easy (that is, as the Spirit of God moves), for as many as 10,000 or more to be baptized with the Holy Spirit in a single service. That which was virtually impossible 50 years ago is altogether possible at present, that is, if the Holy Spirit can move as He so desires to do. So, from that prayer session Saturday afternoon a few days ago, I know that the Lord is going to baptize untold thousands, even hundreds of thousands — maybe even millions — with the Holy Spirit with the evidence of speaking with other tongues in the great move of God, the great harvest that is soon to come.

TO FORGET AND BE FRUITFUL

"And unto Joseph were born two sons before the years of famine came, which Asenath the daughter of Poti-pherah priest of On bore unto him.

"And Joseph called the name of the firstborn Manasseh: For God, said he, has made me forget all my toil, and all my father's house.

"And the name of the second called he Ephraim: For God has caused me to be fruitful in the land of my affliction" (Gen. 41:50-52).

Joseph was given a Gentile wife, which was a type of the Gentile wife given to Christ, for the church is mostly Gentile.

His two sons who were born during the time of the great harvests — Manasseh and Ephraim — are indicative of his spiritual condition. Manasseh means *"forgetfulness,"* while Ephraim means *"fruitfulness."* Faith in God brought Joseph to this place of prominence and position.

In effect, one might say that the names given to the two sons of Joseph portray the spiritual struggle which he endured.

As stated, naming his firstborn Manasseh tells us something. He said, *"for God has made me forget."*

This shows us that it would not have been possible for Joseph to have forgotten what had happened to him — in other words, to allow the terrible scars to be healed as it regarded what his brothers had done to him — unless God had helped him. When man is left to his own strength, he is simply unable to come to this place that he forgets all the pain, suffering, sorrow, and, in fact, the murderous intent of his brothers. As well, the wounds of loved ones are far worse than the wounds of others.

THE HELP OF THE LORD

At the same time, the Lord will help anyone who will sincerely seek His help as it regards such things. Unfortunately, life is not uneventful. The hurts and the harm come, sometimes by those we love the most. In such situations, it is so easy to grow bitter, but if so, we actually hurt no one but ourselves.

Every evidence is Joseph earnestly sought the Lord about this matter. He knew that he didn't have the strength to put this out of his mind, but the Lord answered his prayer and helped him to forget. This tells us what we must do, and it also tells us how it can be done.

When he was able to forget, which means he placed it in the hands of the Lord in its entirety, then he was able to be fruitful. As it held true for Joseph, it holds true for every believer.

We want to be fruitful, and we can be, but only if we forget!

THE FAMINE

"And the seven years of plenteousness, that was in the land of Egypt, were ended.

"And the seven years of famine began to come, according as Joseph had said: and the famine was in all lands; but in all the land of Egypt there was bread" (Gen. 41:53-54).

All of this was for many reasons; however, the great reason at the moment was to bring the brothers of Joseph to Egypt. The ultimate goal as superintended by the Lord was that the entirety of the family of Jacob would come into Egypt, where they would remain for some 215 years before being delivered by the power of God. As we shall see, the family of Jacob numbered 70 when they came into Egypt; they would go out approximately 2.5 to 3 million strong.

THE EXTENT OF THE FAMINE

"And when all the land of Egypt was famished, the people cried to Pharaoh for bread: and Pharaoh said

unto all the Egyptians, Go unto Joseph; what he says to you, do.

"And the famine was over all the face of the earth: And Joseph opened all the storehouses, and sold unto the Egyptians; and the famine waxed sore in the land of Egypt.

"And all countries came into Egypt to Joseph for to buy corn; because that the famine was so sore in all lands" (Gen. 41:55-57).

The great plan of God would include bringing Jacob and his family into Egypt, where, as stated, they would remain for many years before being delivered. Even though they would ultimately be made slaves in that land, all of this — their being in Egypt — would have a tendency to keep them together as a people without them being disseminated into other cultures, which Satan had already tried previously.

However, before the excursion into Egypt could come, there was the matter of reconciliation between Joseph and his brothers. This must be done and, to be sure, would shortly come to pass.

It seems that all evidence points to the fact that these men, who had been so hateful and murderous years before, had now changed. In other words, they were not the same men that Joseph had known some twenty-odd years before. Their reconciliation with Joseph presents one of the most memorable scenes in history, not only for them, but for Jacob, as well, and especially for Jacob.

"Amazing grace! How sweet the sound,
"That saved a wretch like me!
"I once was lost, but now I am found,
"Was blind, but now I see."

"'Twas grace that taught my heart to fear,
"And grace my fears relieved;
"How precious did that grace appear
"The hour I first believed."

"Through many dangers, toils, and snares,
"I have already come;
"'Tis grace has brought me safe thus far,
"And grace will lead me home."

"When we've been there ten thousand years,
"Bright shining as the sun,
"We've no less days to sing God's praise
  "Than when we first begun."

JOSEPH

CHAPTER

8

BENJAMIN

CHAPTER EIGHT

BENJAMIN

"And Joseph's ten brethren went down to buy corn in Egypt.

"But Benjamin, Joseph's brother, Jacob sent not with his brethren; for he said, Lest peradventure mischief befall him.

"And the sons of Israel came to buy corn among those who came: for the famine was in the land of Canaan" (Gen. 42:3-5).

Both Joseph and Benjamin were the sons of Rachel and, thereby, special to Jacob. Even though he loved all his sons, it seems that these were the only two who truly served the Lord, at least at this particular time.

Quite possibly, Jacob mused in his heart that with Joseph now being dead, or so he thought, the Lord would place the mantle on Benjamin; therefore, he would specifically watch over the young man, who was now about 20 years of age.

The Lord had not revealed to Jacob that these were His plans, but Jacob, not knowing what had actually happened, at least as it regarded Joseph, could only see Benjamin taking

Joseph's place. So, he would not allow him to go into Egypt with his brothers.

JOSEPH

"And Joseph was the governor over the land, and he it was who sold to all the people of the land: and Joseph's brethren came, and bowed down themselves before him with their faces to the earth" (Gen. 42:6).

Had Joseph thought of his own dignity and of his own affection, he would have revealed himself at once to his brothers; however, such a revelation would have produced confusion but not repentance. He loved them and, therefore, sought their spiritual welfare.

As we shall see, he still concealed himself from them. This was so their sin would be brought to their remembrance and make them confess it with their own lips, and not just to him in his presence, but to God in His presence.

In all of this we see how God deals with us as it regards repentance. For repentance to truly be repentance, it must always be sincere and total.

Joseph had been governor now for eight years before he saw the fulfillment of the dreams he had as a 17-year-old boy.

The day finally arrived that the sons of Jacob came to Egypt and, thereby, to Joseph in order to purchase grain. They bowed down themselves to him as the lord of Egypt, but did not recognize him as their brother whom they had sold as a slave more than 20 years before.

Why didn't Joseph reveal himself to his brethren then? In fact, why didn't Joseph contact his brothers and his father once becoming prime minister of Egypt? He had the means to do so, and in grand style.

Joseph was doing what the Lord wanted him to do. If his brothers had not changed, a meeting with them would have done little good. He had to determine if they were still the same men they had been, or if time had effected a change, all brought about by the Lord.

Joseph had most definitely forgiven his brothers, but the circle couldn't be complete until they truly repented of their former actions toward him. There is a great lesson in all of this for us.

FORGIVENESS

The believer is to instantly forgive anyone who wrongs him in any way. He is to do this for several reasons, the least not being that Christ has forgiven us of so much more than we are called upon to forgive others. Also, if we have truly been forgiven ourselves — which refers to being born again and truly living for God — we will always remember what the Lord has done for us and be quick to forgive others.

As well, our forgiving others keeps down bitterness in our own hearts and, in fact, is more so for our good than the one to whom we are extending forgiveness. This means that we are to forgive them even though they are wrong in what they have done, that is, if they are, even though they have not asked for forgiveness.

Jesus said: *"For if you forgive men their trespasses, your heavenly Father will also forgive you:*

"But if you forgive not men their trespasses, neither will your Father forgive your trespasses" (Mat. 6:14-15).

As should be obvious, there is a severe penalty here that is attached to the failure to forgive.

We must understand, as well, that the type of forgiveness we extend to others must be the same type of forgiveness that God has extended to us. It cannot be a partial or half-hearted forgiveness. It must be total and complete with no conditions attached. If conditions are attached, then this of which we are being engaged is not truly forgiveness but something else altogether.

FELLOWSHIP?

We know that Joseph had definitely forgiven his brothers because of the names given to his two sons. Still, we find here that even though he, who was a type of Christ, had forgiven them, he did not jump into their arms the moment that he saw them. In fact, even as we shall see, he submitted them to a very strenuous test before revealing himself as their brother. What does this mean?

If someone has wronged us and has not asked for our forgiveness, as stated, we are to forgive them just the same; however, this doesn't mean that we are to have fellowship with them. In fact, it's impossible to have fellowship with someone who hasn't truly repented. While we hold nothing in our hearts against them, at the same time, there is no ground for fellowship, as would be obvious. What good would it have done Joseph to reveal himself to his brothers if they were the same men as before? While they may have paid him lip service simply because he was the governor of Egypt, their hearts would have been toward him the same as before, which could only be described as a murderous heart. Let it ever be understood that this entire scenario is a perfect picture of evildoings within the church. These men had murder in their hearts toward Joseph. Any time we do something harmful to a fellow brother or sister in Christ, we are engaging a murderous heart toward them. We should remember that.

HIS BRETHREN

"And Joseph saw his brethren, and he knew them, but made himself strange unto them, and spoke roughly unto them; and he said unto them, From where do you come? And they said, From the land of Canaan to buy food.

"And Joseph knew his brethren, but they knew not him" (Gen. 42:7-8).

As Joseph (a type of Christ) was ruler over Egypt, likewise, the Lord Jesus Christ is ruler over all. In fact, it is Christ who is the source of all blessings in the United States and elsewhere. Consequently, when Israel accepts help from this country, whether she realizes it or not, she is bowing to the Lord Jesus Christ.

Verse 7 says that Joseph *"spoke roughly unto them."* In the great tribulation period, the Lord Jesus Christ will deal roughly with Israel. It will be called the *"time of Jacob's trouble"* *(Jer. 30:7).*

Verse 8 proclaims the fact that while Joseph knew his brethren, they didn't know him. Christ knows Israel, but sadly, *they know not Him.*

Joseph's dealings with his brothers is a picture of the future action of the Lord Jesus Christ in bringing Israel to recognize her sin and rejection of Him, and the consequent enormity of that sin against God. As we have stated, had Joseph only been concerned about his own dignity, he would have revealed himself at once to his brothers. He had the power to do so, as would be obvious, and there was nothing they could do in any capacity, him being the governor of all of Egypt.

Likewise, Christ could easily reveal Himself presently to Israel, and do so immediately. However, as such revelation would have produced only confusion among Joseph's brethren, likewise, such revelation by Christ to Israel could, as well, only produce confusion. There has to be biblical repentance before there can be a glorious revelation.

THE DREAMS

"And Joseph remembered the dreams which he dreamed of them, and said unto them, You are spies; to see the nakedness of the land you are come" (Gen. 42:9).

As these men bowed before Joseph, the dream that he had when only 17 years old now flashed before him. It was being fulfilled before his eyes. As someone has well said, *"The mills of God grind slowly, but they grind exceedingly fine."* In other words, the mills of God miss nothing!

Now begins the first procedure toward their repentance. He accused them of being spies, which was a most serious charge! What would they say to this charge? Their answer would reveal much about themselves.

THEIR ANSWER

"And they said unto him, No, my lord, but to buy food are your servants come.

"We are all one man's sons; we are true men, your servants are no spies.

"And he said unto them, No, but to see the nakedness of the land you are come.

"And they said, Your servants are twelve brethren, the sons of one man in the land of Canaan; and, behold, the youngest is this day with our father, and one is not.

"And Joseph said unto them, That is it that I spoke unto you, saying, You are spies:

"Hereby you shall be proved: By the life of Pharaoh you shall not go forth hence, except your youngest brother come hither" (Gen. 42:10-15).

The day the brothers of Joseph came before him, no doubt, there were many other people present, as well. They were all there from various countries to buy food. So, it must have seemed peculiar to the brothers of Joseph for him to single them out. Incidentally, he spoke to them in Egyptian, with his words translated to them by someone else.

YOU ARE SPIES?

He had only been 17 years of age when they saw him last. He was now about 38. As well, he was dressed as an Egyptian, so they had no inkling of knowledge that this was Joseph.

Abruptly, he said to them, *"You are spies."* The charge was extremely serious, but yet, common sense would tell all concerned that if, in fact, their intention was spying, the entire family would not have come on such a mission. Irrespective, they were helpless before him.

They denied the accusations, and rightly so, and claimed to be true men, i.e., honest men. They then revealed some things about themselves: They were 10 of the 12 sons of one man. One was at home, and the other was not, meaning that in their minds, Joseph was dead.

More than 20 years had passed since that fateful day of so long before, and they had not heard from Joseph in all of this time, so they reasoned that he was dead. Little did they realize that the man standing before them was indeed Joseph!

Reasoning that Jacob had probably transferred the birthright to Benjamin, he wanted to know the attitude of these men toward Benjamin, so he proved them.

PRISON

*"Send one of you, and let him fetch your brother, and
you shall be kept in prison, that your words may be proved,
whether there be any truth in you: or else by the life of Pharaoh surely you are spies"* (Gen. 42:16).

Joseph's detention of Simeon and afterwards of Benjamin were skillfully designed so as to find out if they still were
indifferent to the cries of a captive brother and the tears of a
bereaved father.

He proposed to keep nine of the brothers in prison, while
one went back to their respective homes in order to fetch Benjamin. This must have come like a bombshell to them as he
spoke to them through an interpreter.

In a sense, all of these men were types of Christ, but in a
very limited way. As we've already stated, the meaning of their
names points to Christ and what He will do for dying humanity.

Both Joseph and Benjamin were types of Christ in a much
more pronounced way, and especially Joseph. Joseph's name
means *"the Lord will add,"* and Benjamin's name means
"a strong right arm." Both meanings put together say,
"The Lord will add a strong right arm." It refers not only
to Joseph being the saviour of his family, as well as so many
others during that trying time in Egypt of so long ago, but
more than all, of the One of whom he was a type. In the great
tribulation that is yet to come, the Lord Jesus Christ, who is
the strong right arm of the Father, will save Israel from the
wicked hands of the Antichrist.

GOD

"And he put them all together into ward three days.

"And Joseph said unto them the third day, This do, and live; for I fear God" (Gen. 42:17-18).

Fear must have played havoc in the minds of these men as they were placed under detention for three days. At this point, they had no idea as to what would happen next.

At the end of three days, Joseph came to them with his interpreter. He would now make a different proposal to them and would begin this proposal by evoking the name of Elohim.

Knowing and understanding Egypt and its worship of many gods, and knowing that Egypt little knew Jehovah, if at all, what must they have thought when Joseph proclaimed to them through the interpreter that he knew and feared Elohim, who, in fact, was the God of the Hebrews?

All of this had to be extremely strange to them because they knew that Elohim was little known, if at all, outside of their respective family. Even though Joseph was speaking through an interpreter, and even though he may himself have used the Egyptian word for the supreme deity, doubtless he would take care that the interpreter used the word *Elohim*, i.e., *God*.

By Joseph proclaiming the fact that he feared God, in essence, he was saying to them that he would not do anything that would be displeasing to God. So, they had nothing to fear as it regarded the safety of the one left behind, which he would now demand.

Would to Heaven that every leader in the world feared God, but the sad truth is, precious few hold any fear of God whatsoever.

An excellent portrayal of this is found in the actions, attitude, and spirit of America. For instance, the recent situation in Afghanistan, in effect, puts Christianity up beside Islam, at least after a fashion. We find care and concern for the lives and welfare of others in the actions of American soldiers. Little of that, if any, is found among those who fight for Islam. In fact, life is cheap in that false religion.

The United States, while having many faults, still retains a semblance of the fear of God. That and that alone serves as the foundation of all truth. In Islam, there is no truth, only that which is instigated by Satan, which is a lie, because Satan is a liar and the father of all lies (Jn. 8:44).

THE PROPOSAL

"If you be true men, let one of your brethren be bound in the house of your prison: go you, carry corn for the famine of your houses:

"But bring your youngest brother unto me; so shall your words be verified, and you shall not die. And they did so" (Gen. 42:19-20).

Joseph now softened his demands in that he had first stated that nine of the brothers would remain in Egypt while one was sent to fetch Benjamin, but now, he limited that to just one remaining in Egypt while the nine went back home.

As well, he told them to take grain back home. How different this was than when they had intended to leave him in a pit in order to starve. Actually, he now only had two demands:

1. Simeon must remain in Egypt.
2. When they returned to buy more grain, Benjamin must come with them.

All of this was designed by the Holy Spirit. Joseph wanted to assure himself that Benjamin was well. In fact, having been sold into Egypt shortly before Benjamin was born, he had never seen his younger brother.

THE SIN

"And they said one to another, We are verily guilty concerning our brother, in that we saw the anguish of his soul, when he besought us, and we would not hear; therefore is this distress come upon us.

"And Reuben answered them, saying, Did I not speak unto you, saying, Do not sin against the child; and you would not hear? therefore, behold, also his blood is required.

"And they knew not that Joseph understood them; for he spoke unto them by an interpreter.

"And he turned himself about from them, and wept; and returned to them again, and communed with them, and took from them Simeon, and bound him before their eyes" (Gen. 42:21-24).

Upon hearing this demand by Joseph that one brother must be left behind, and knowing that this must be done, the men began to speak among themselves, not knowing that Joseph could understand them. We find in this Israel's actions in the latter days. As these men, they will be called to pass through deep and searching trial and through intensely painful exercises of conscience.

ISRAEL AND THE SECOND COMING OF CHRIST

Israel will think the Antichrist is the Messiah. I must believe that in the coming great tribulation when the Antichrist will turn on them, Israel will think long and hard regarding the Lord Jesus Christ, especially considering that 144,000 will come to Christ at that time. I cannot see how that it can be otherwise.

This one thing is certain: the moment that Christ returns, which will take place at the second coming and will be in power and glory such as the world has never experienced, Israel will accept him immediately (Rev., Chpt. 19; Zech., Chpts. 13-14).

The first thing that the sons of Jacob thought about, as it regarded what was demanded of them, was the sin they committed against their brother, little knowing that he was standing before them. They said, *"We are verily guilty."*

Joseph had earnestly besought them not to do the terrible thing they were doing when they sold him to the Ishmaelites, but they would not hear. The idea that they graphically recalled the anguish of his soul at that awful time points to the biting conscience.

Irrespective as to how long it has been, unless sin is duly repented of before God and forsaken, its biting torment will not go away. This is the reason for much physical breakdown, and worse yet, emotional distress that plagues humanity. It is sin that lies heavily upon the soul of the individual.

HIS BLOOD IS REQUIRED

Reuben now reminded them that he had asked them not to sin against Joseph, but they would not hear — all of this after some twenty-odd years.

Then he said, *"Behold, also his blood is required,"* meaning that they surmised that Joseph was dead. So, now they were going to have to pay.

God had said to Noah so long, long before, *"Whoso sheds man's blood (cold blood), by man shall his blood be shed: for in the image of God made He man"* (Gen. 9:6).

Because of man's terrible spiritual condition, the Lord Jesus Christ would have to shed His life's blood, which alone could atone for the sins of man. Paul said, *"But now in Christ Jesus you who sometimes were far off are made near by the blood of Christ"* (Eph. 2:13).

John said, *"And the blood of Jesus Christ His Son cleanses us from all sin"* (I Jn. 1:7).

The human race has sinned against God and against man, and as such, atonement had to be made. It was Christ alone who could make such atonement, and He did by the giving of Himself in sacrifice, which necessitated the pouring out of His own precious blood. That's why Peter said: *"Forasmuch as you know that you were not redeemed with corruptible things, as silver and gold ... But with the precious blood of Christ, as of a lamb without blemish and without spot"* (I Pet. 1:18-19).

MAN WILL ANSWER

Man has a choice: He can answer to God, or he can answer to Christ. If he answers to Christ, this means that he accepts Christ and what Christ did for us at the Cross as the sacrifice and will, thereby, be saved. Refusing that, he will have to answer to God, which speaks of the great white throne judgment, and means to be lost forever and forever (Rev. 20:11-15).

As they spoke among themselves, Joseph turned away from them and wept. As stated, they didn't know that he understood what they said. He wept simply because he knew that they were coming close to true repentance.

He then took Simeon and bound him before their eyes, which meant that he was the one who must be left behind. Why Simeon was chosen, we aren't told. More than likely, he was the ringleader in the terrible sin that had been committed against Joseph those long years earlier.

"Nor silver nor gold has attained my redemption,
"Nor riches of earth could have saved my poor soul;
"The blood of the Cross is my only foundation,
"The death of my Saviour now makes me whole."

"Nor silver nor gold has attained my redemption,
"The guilt on my conscience too heavy had grown;
"The blood of the Cross is my only foundation,
"The death of my Saviour could only atone."

"Nor silver nor gold has attained my redemption,
"The holy commandment forbade me draw near;
"The blood of the Cross is my only foundation,
"The death of my Saviour removes my fear."

"Nor silver nor gold has attained my redemption,
"The way into Heaven could not thus be bought;
"The blood of the Cross is my only foundation,
"The death of my Saviour redemption has wrought."

JOSEPH

CHAPTER

9

JOSEPH AND HIS BROTHERS

CHAPTER NINE

JOSEPH AND HIS BROTHERS

PROVISION

"Then Joseph commanded to fill their sacks with corn, and to restore every man's money into his sack, and to give them provision for the way: and thus did he unto them" (Gen. 42:25).

The word corn should have been translated *"grain."* There was no corn as we know such in that part of the world at that time. To our knowledge, corn was first known by the pilgrims in America, which they learned from the Indians.

I would dare say that the story of Joseph and his brothers is the most remarkable incident in human history. I do not think that anything can even remotely equal the drama of such a happening.

Joseph was sold into Egypt as a slave, and now he was the governor of the entirety of the nation of Egypt, the greatest on the face of the earth. This means that he was the second most powerful man in the world. His brothers did not have the faintest idea that the man with whom they had been deal-ing was indeed their brother Joseph.

The reason it is so remarkable is because Joseph was a type of Christ, and this which happened to him was a por-trayal of what Israel would do to Christ. As Joseph was sold for 20 pieces of silver, likewise, Christ was sold for 30 pieces of silver. As Joseph's brothers hated him, likewise, Israel, the brethren of Christ, hated Him. As Joseph became the gover-nor of Egypt, which was Gentile, likewise, Jesus is the Head of the church, which is by and large Gentile. As Joseph would save his brothers from starvation, as well, Christ will save Israel during the coming great tribulation, although behind the scenes. As the brothers of Joseph finally accepted him, likewise, Israel will ultimately accept Christ.

WHAT HAS GOD DONE?

"And they loaded their donkeys with the corn (grain), *and departed thence.*

"And as one of them opened his sack to give his donkey provender in the inn, he espied (saw) *his money; for, behold, it was in his sack's mouth.*

"And he said unto his brethren, My money is restored; and, lo, it is even in my sack: and their heart failed them, and they were afraid, saying one to another, What is this that God has done unto us?" (Gen. 42:26-28).

Actually they were right! It was God who was guid-ing these events, giving Joseph instructions all along the way as to how he should handle the situation. However, because of their sin — a sin committed well over 20 years before — they were thinking of God in a very negative way. It is no different presently.

Most all of the world totally and completely misunderstands God. The guilt of sin accompanies every single person who doesn't know Christ, or even the Christian who has failed to repent of his sin. Because of the guilt of sin, such people think that God is out to get them. Any negative thing that happens, or even that which on the surface seems to be negative, is attributed to God.

This is the guilt that caused Adam and Eve to hide from God after they had sinned (Gen. 3:9-10).

THE CROSS

There is only one way for the guilt of sin to be removed and the power of sin to be broken, and that is by and through what Jesus did for us at the Cross. Let the reader understand that there are no exceptions to this. It is the Cross and the Cross alone that can address this problem.

Paul said: *"Knowing this, that our old man is crucified with Him* (what Jesus did for us at the Cross), *that the body of* (the) *sin might be destroyed* (made ineffective), *that henceforth we should not serve* (the) *sin" (Rom. 6:6).*

If the reader is to notice, I have added the word *the* in front of the word *sin*. Actually, this is the way it was originally written by Paul. In other words, the definite article *the* is placed in front of the word *sin,* signifying that Paul was not speaking of acts of sin, but rather the sin nature.

The destruction of the sin nature means here that it becomes inoperative. It no longer holds sway in our lives as it did before we were born again. While it does remain with us, even as Paul roundly proclaims in Romans, Chapter 6, it is to be dormant. In fact, it will be dormant if our faith is placed exclusively in the Cross and remains in the Cross. The Holy Spirit demands that (Rom. 8:1-11).

FAITH

With our faith placed exclusively in the finished work of Christ, as stated, the guilt of sin is removed and the power of sin is broken. These two things are the greatest things that could ever happen to any human being. With guilt being gone, which can only happen by the Cross and our faith in that finished work, peace then reigns. With the power of sin broken, we can then yield our *"members as instruments of righteousness unto God" (Rom. 6:13).* Once we were controlled by the sin nature, but now the sin nature is controlled by us. The *divine nature* is now in control, which comes into the heart and life of every believer at conversion.

Concerning this, Peter said: *"Whereby are given unto us exceeding great and precious promises: that by these you might be partakers of the divine nature, having escaped the corruption that is in the world through lust"* (II Pet. 1:4).

With the divine nature now controlling us, which is, in effect, the Holy Spirit and His work, we know that God has only good things for us. In fact, that is true regarding God and all of humanity, but, as stated, due to the guilt of sin, men do not think of God in a positive fashion.

JACOB

"And they came unto Jacob their father unto the land of Canaan, and told him all that befell unto them; saying,

"The man, who is the lord of the land, spoke roughly to us, and took us for spies of the country.

"And we said unto him, We are true men; we are no spies:

"We be twelve brethren, sons of our father; one is not, and the youngest is this day with our father in the land of Canaan.

"And the man, the lord of the country, said unto us, Hereby shall I know that you are true men; leave one of your brethren here with me, and take food for the famine of your households, and be gone:

"And bring your youngest brother unto me: then shall I know that you are no spies, but that you are true men: so will I deliver you your brother, and you shall traffick in the land" (Gen. 42:29-34).

From the terminology used by these men at this present time, it is obvious that a change had taken place in their lives; however, it was a change that was not quite yet complete.

COME CLEAN

For instance, their terminology was as it ought to be, in other words, they spoke now with an entirely different spirit than they did those twenty-odd years before when they sold Joseph. Still, they had not yet completely come clean with God and their father Jacob concerning what they had done.

As far as Jacob knew, Joseph was dead, killed by a wild animal. That's what his sons had told him, and they had never rectified this thing as of yet.

However, as we shall see, the Holy Spirit would force them into a position to where they had to come clean. He will do the same with every single believer, even presently, because sin can only be handled in one way, and that is by proper confession. What does that mean?

It means that we confess our sin to God, and do so unequivocally (I Jn. 1:9). As well, we must confess to every single person we have wronged and seek their forgiveness.

James said: *"Confess your faults one to another, and pray one for another, that you may be healed"* (James 5:16).

Unfortunately, millions of Christians, and I speak in the present tense, do not properly follow this scriptural admonition. They try to justify their actions, whatever those actions may be. Proper justification, however, can only be brought about by proper confession to the Lord and to those we have wronged.

FEAR

"And it came to pass as they emptied their sacks, that, behold, every man's bundle of money was in his sack: and when both they and their father saw the bundles of money, they were afraid" (Gen. 42:35).

They now feared, and for many things. What did it mean that their money had been restored unto them in the sacks of grain?

Actually, there was no way they could do this themselves, but why would the lord of Egypt have done this, or so they reasoned in their minds. Actually, why did Joseph give them back their money, charging them nothing for the grain?

While Joseph was definitely taking stern measures to assure himself of the change in his brothers, at the same time, he held in his heart nothing but good for them.

Even when the Lord is forced to chastise us, as He does all believers, during the chastisement, He always does good things for us at different intervals. That's the reason, or at least one of the reasons, that it is such a joy to live for the Lord. Even when He is stern, as He sometimes must be, He is at the same time tender.

JOSEPH

"And the men took that present, and they took double money in their hand, and Benjamin; and rose up, and went down to Egypt, and stood before Joseph" (Gen. 43:15).

All the food obtained on their first journey was now gone. So they must now go back to Egypt to secure more grain because the famine was very sore in the land.

But yet, Joseph, whom they did not recognize as Joseph, had demanded that when they came back, they must bring their younger brother Benjamin with them. Upon hearing this, Jacob was nonplussed to say the least. At first, he rejected the idea altogether.

However, when the situation became acute, with food becoming more and more scarce, finally, he had to relent and allow Benjamin to go. He had no choice.

The brothers now came back to Egypt with Benjamin, and they stood before Joseph, but the thing is, they did not know it was Joseph.

They had brought double money, payment for the previous purchase and for the present purchase. As well, they had their gift for Joseph. All of this was to prove that they were honest men. Little did they realize what Joseph's intentions actually were.

The Scripture says, *"and stood before Joseph."* He was their brother and their saviour, but yet, they did not know him. Likewise, Israel will stand before Christ at the second coming and will not know Him. They will ask, *"What are these wounds in Your hands?"* Then He shall answer, *"Those with which I was wounded in the house of My friends"* (Zech. 13:6).

BENJAMIN

"And when Joseph saw Benjamin with them, he said to the ruler of his house, Bring these men home, and kill, and make ready; for these men shall dine with me at noon.

"And the man did as Joseph bade; and the man brought the men into Joseph's house.

"And the men were afraid, because they were brought into Joseph's house; and they said, Because of the money that was returned in our sacks at the first time are we brought in; that he may seek occasion against us, and fall upon us, and take us for bondmen, and our donkeys" (Gen. 43:16-18).

The union of Benjamin with Joseph points forward to the day when Christ, as Benjamin, will be the Son of the right hand to Israel, and as Joseph, king over all the earth.

The brothers arrived and stood before Joseph, and he saw his younger brother Benjamin, who, most probably, he had never seen before. Benjamin was probably born a little while after Joseph had been sold into Egypt. Once again, events became strange and unexplainable to the brothers.

They were to be brought to the house of Joseph, which, no doubt, was a very palatial affair. As these men in their crude shepherd's garments were ushered in, they could only imagine something negative. Perhaps they were under arrest, and the first thing that went through their minds was the money that they found in their sacks which they had paid for the first purchase. They all imagined themselves being arrested.

THE STEWARD

"And they came near to the steward of Joseph's house, and they communed with him at the door of the house,

"And said, O sir, we came indeed down at the first time to buy food:

"And it came to pass, when we came to the inn, that we opened our sacks, and, behold, every man's money was in the mouth of his sack, our money in full weight: and we have brought it again in our hand.

"And other money have we brought down in our hands to buy food: we cannot tell who put our money in our sacks.

"And he said, Peace be to you, fear not: your God, and the God of your father, has given you treasure in your sacks: I had your money. And he brought Simeon out unto them" (Gen. 43:19-23).

The conduct of Joseph cannot be explained except on the grounds of his inspiration. He was not acting. He was not trifling with human feelings. He was not merely following the dictate of his own personal affections. He was, under divine direction, planning for the removal of his father's house to Egypt, that the people of God may pass through their season of trial in the house of bondage.

The tenderness, pathos, simplicity, and truthfulness — especially in the case of Joseph — proclaim the criteria of real greatness. The Bible histories help us to keep in mind that real salvation does not suppress but preserves and develops all that is best and noblest in man.

Joseph's dealings with his brothers gradually prepared their minds for the great announcement that was soon to be made.

Evidently this steward could speak Hebrew, or else, an interpreter was present, which was most likely the case. At any rate, the brothers began to explain to him the situation regarding the money that had been placed in their sacks on their first visit.

STRANGE!

It seems that the steward listened patiently and then simply said something that must have sounded strange to their ears. He spoke of Elohim, whom the Egyptians did not know. So, it seems that Joseph had taught his steward to fear and trust the God of the Hebrews.

And yet, there is no indication that this man knew that these men standing before him were indeed the flesh and blood brothers of Joseph. However, he was perfectly aware that they were innocent in the matter of the money. In fact, he related to them that he was the one who had placed the money in their sacks.

All of this must have been exceedingly strange to them. *"What could all of it mean?"* they must have asked themselves.

Then Simeon was brought out to them, and none the worse for wear.

There is no indication whatsoever that Joseph communed with Simeon at all during those months of waiting for the brothers to return.

THE GIFT

"And the man brought the men into Joseph's house, and gave them water, and they washed their feet; and he gave their donkeys provender.

"And they made ready the present against Joseph came at noon: for they heard that they should eat bread there.

"And when Joseph came home, they brought him the present which was in their hand into the house, and bowed themselves to him to the earth" (Gen. 43:24-26).

The further it went, the stranger it became.

Surely the lord of Egypt didn't invite rank strangers from other nations of the earth into his house to eat with him, and especially lowly shepherds! But yet, here they were.

The steward had spoken kindly to them, as well. Simeon had been restored, and this somewhat allayed their fears.

One thing is certain: They were not accustomed to the luxury and opulence of their surroundings. In fact, they had probably never seen such. Then Joseph came into the room.

They brought him the gift that they had prepared and then *"bowed themselves to him to the earth,"* again fulfilling his dream.

THE QUESTIONS

"And he asked them of their welfare, and said, Is your father well, the old man of whom you spoke? Is he yet alive?

"And they answered, Your servant our father is in good health, he is yet alive. And they bowed down their heads, and made obeisance" (Gen. 43:27-28).

It must have seemed unusual to the sons of Jacob to hear the lord of Egypt asking personal questions about their father, his health, etc. However, according to the protocol of that time, they did not dare question this ruler of Egypt.

When Joseph asked this question concerning his father Jacob, it had been approximately 21 years since he had seen Jacob.

As well, we must understand Joseph's caution. Twenty-one years before, these men were murderers, that is, with the exception of Benjamin, who had not yet been born. The great question concerned what they were now! Consequently, Joseph's actions were designed to draw out their true character, and that it would. He would find that they were now changed men.

What had effected that change, we aren't told; however, it was now obvious that they were different men with different attitudes. One might say that in the meantime, they had been *born again.*

"In the misty days of yore
"Jesus' precious blood had power
"Even the thief on the cross to save
"Like a bird his spirit flies
"To its home in Paradise,
"Through the power of Calvary's crimson wave."

"I was lost and steeped in guilt,
"But the blood for sinners spilt
"Washed away my sins and set me free;
"Now and evermore the same,
"Praise, O praise His holy name!
"Will the cleansing stream availing be."

"God in mercy ask you why,
"Brother sinner, will you die
"When such full redemption He provides?
"You have but to look and live,
"Life eternal He will give,
"For the power of Calvary still abides."

"Bring your burdens, come today,
"Turn from all your sins away,
"He can fully save and sanctify;
"From the wrath to come, now flee,
"Let your name recorded be
 "With the blood-washed and redeemed on high."

JOSEPH

CHAPTER

10

JOSEPH AND BENJAMIN

CHAPTER TEN

JOSEPH AND BENJAMIN

"And he lifted up his eyes, and saw his brother Benjamin, his mother's son, and said, Is this your younger brother, of whom you spoke unto me? And he said, God be gracious unto you, my son" (Gen. 43:29).

As stated, this was the first time that Joseph had seen Benjamin. He had not yet been born when Joseph was sold into Egypt. The other men were Joseph's half-brothers, meaning that Jacob was their father, but they had different mothers. Benjamin's father was Jacob, even as Jacob was the father of them all, but his mother was Rachel, the mother of Joseph also.

The brothers had heard the steward of Joseph use the name of Elohim, and now they heard Joseph saying the same thing, *"God* (Elohim) *be gracious unto you, my son,"* as he spoke to Benjamin. These were the first words that he said to the much younger boy. The tenderness of his terminology must have been extremely encouraging to all who were there.

WEEPING

"And Joseph made haste; for his bowels did yearn upon his brother: and he sought where to weep; and he entered into his chamber, and wept there.

"And he washed his face, and went out, and refrained himself, and said, Set on bread" (Gen. 43:30-31).

As Joseph looked at his younger brother, he was overcome by emotion, but yet, as the governor of Egypt, he couldn't let his brothers see him weeping because they simply wouldn't understand. So, he slipped out of the room where they all had gathered, and went into another room where he could be alone, and the Scripture says, *"and wept there."*

The scene was poignant not only as it expressed the feelings of the moment, but it presents itself in a much larger way, even as it typifies that coming day when Christ will stand before Israel. At long last the sons of Jacob will have come home. In fact, in all of history there has never been anything so drastic as the fall of Jacob, and I speak of the nation of Israel and their rejection of Christ. It eclipses every other happening.

Paul said: *"For if the casting away of them* (Israel) *be the reconciling of the world, what shall the receiving of them be, but life from the dead?"* (Rom. 11:15).

Their fall has been so drastic, so all-encompassing, so total, and so complete that it will take the great tribulation to finally bring them to their senses. The great Prophet Jeremiah referred to it as *"the time of Jacob's trouble,"* but then he said, *"but he shall be saved out of it"* (Jer. 30:7).

Finally, broken and humbled just as the ancient sons of Jacob, they will stand before Christ. However, then, exactly as Joseph, He will not be the lowly Nazarene, the meek and lowly One, but rather the King of kings and the Lord of lords.

THE FELLOWSHIP

"And they set on for him by himself, and for them by themselves, and for the Egyptians, which did eat with him, by themselves: because the Egyptians might not eat bread with the Hebrews; for that is an abomination unto the Egyptians.

"And they sat before him, the firstborn according to his birthright, and the youngest according to his youth: and the men marvelled one at another.

"And he took and sent messes unto them from before him: but Benjamin's mess was five times as much as any of theirs. And they drank, and were merry with him" (Gen. 43:32-34).

The meal presented here was indicative of that which will take place at the second coming when both Jews and Gentiles will fellowship with Christ, of whom Joseph was a type.

They marveled that he knew their ages and seated them accordingly. *"How could he know this?"* they must have reasoned. Christ knows all things.

Benjamin was given five times as much food as the others, portraying the grace of God, for the number five is God's number of grace.

The brothers were now thrust into an arrangement of luxury they had never previously known. In the first place,

Egyptians didn't eat with Hebrews, or any other national-ity for that matter, considering themselves to be superior. It was a matter of their religious beliefs. So, the brothers ate by themselves, with Joseph eating with the Egyptians, who now considered Joseph as one of their own.

STRANGE HAPPENINGS

However, when the brothers of Joseph were assigned their places regarding the meal, as stated, they were astounded that he seated them according to their ages. Reuben was the first-born, while Benjamin was the youngest, with all the others seated according to their ages. *"How did Joseph know this?"* they must have reasoned? The Scripture says, *"they mar-veled,"* and no wonder!

As well, whenever the food was brought, Benjamin received five times as much as the others. Once again, they must have been astounded as to why Joseph had this carried out.

There was a scriptural reason for this action. First of all, as stated, five is the number of the grace of God. For instance, Christ was given five names by the Holy Spirit (Isa. 9:6). As well, He suffered five wounds at the Crucifixion:

1. Whipped
2. Nails in the hands
3. Nails in the feet
4. Thorns in the brow
5. Spear in the side

Also, there is a fivefold calling: apostles, prophets, evangelists, pastors, and teachers (Eph. 4:11).

The name *Benjamin* means *"my strong right hand,"* typifying Christ. In a coming day when Israel comes back to Christ, even though Christ has a strong right hand, He will deal with Israel in grace. This was signified by the food given to Benjamin, which was five times more than that given to his brothers.

THE SILVER CUP

"And he commanded the steward of his house, saying, Fill the men's sacks with food, as much as they can carry, and put every man's money in his sack's mouth.

"And put my cup, the silver cup, in the sack's mouth of the youngest, and his corn money. And he did according to the word that Joseph had spoken" (Gen. 44:1-2).

The casual reader may think that Joseph was being somewhat harsh respecting this next episode; however, two things must be remembered:

1. Joseph was being led by the Lord in all that he did here.
2. Due to the enormity of the sin of these brothers, with the exception of Benjamin, he had to make certain that there had been true repentance in their hearts. Everything was at stake, and I speak of the future of the nation of Israel. If it were founded on murder and deceit, it could not survive. It must be founded on true repentance before God, hence, Joseph taking the stern measure that he took.

THE FINAL PART OF THE PLAN

"As soon as the morning was light, the men were sent away, they and their donkeys.

"And when they were gone out of the city, and not yet far off, Joseph said unto his steward, Up, follow after the men; and when you do overtake them, say unto them, Wherefore have you rewarded evil for good?

"Is not this it in which my lord drinks, and whereby indeed he divines? you have done evil in so doing.

"And he overtook them, and he spoke unto them these same words" (Gen. 44:3-6).

If it is to be noticed, in all of this, these brothers were guilty of many dreadful sins, and these are recorded in the sacred text, but they only thought of this one great commanding sin, the rejection of their brother Joseph.

Some sins are worse than others, and what they did was the worst sin of all, hence, it weighed heavily on their hearts.

None can teach like God. He alone can produce in the conscience the true sense of sin and bring the soul down into the profound depths of its own condition in His presence. In fact, in everything that was being done, the Lord was guiding Joseph.

Men run on in their career of guilt, heedless of everything, until the arrow of the Almighty pierces their conscience. Then they are led into those searchings of heart and intensive exercises of soul, which can only find relief in the rich resources of redeeming love.

The sin of these brothers was exceedingly bad, not only because it was a sin against their own flesh and blood, but primarily because it was a sin against God's will. It was the Lord who selected Joseph for the birthright. Their actions prove that they despised what was done, which meant that their anger was actually against God.

SIN

While all sin is in some way against God, some sins strike directly at the throat of His will, hence, they are sins of great magnitude. In fact, the sins of Paul fell into that category. Before he was saved, he greatly opposed the will of God by opposing those who had accepted Christ. When it comes down to the bottom line, all sin in one way or the other is in opposition to Christ and what He did for us at the Cross. There rests every sin, every transgression, all iniquity, etc.

The fact of guilt does not have to be determined as it regards sin because that is obvious. All sin carries with it its own guilt. It is repentance that must be tested, and as always, it is tested by one's faith and in no other way.

Had these men truly repented? Every evidence says they had, and I speak of their attitude, their actions, their spirit; however, many will act one way in one place and another way some place else. In the face of Joseph with his commanding authority, what else could they do? So, he had to do one final thing to prove to himself that what he hoped was evident in their lives was in fact the truth. The test was now underway.

A DECLARATION OF INNOCENCE

"And they said unto him, Wherefore says my lord these words? God forbid that your servants should do according to this thing:

"Behold, the money, which we found in our sacks' mouths, we brought again unto you out of the land of Canaan: how then should we steal out of your lord's house silver or gold?

"With whomsoever of your servants it be found, both let him die, and we also will be my lord's bondmen" (Gen. 44:7-9).

Events would prove true repentance, and events would also prove a false repentance. We greatly see the grace of God in all of this, and it is beautiful to behold. We also find in all of this that to the faithful heart, God can even turn evil into good while never condoning the evil.

Once again, we find that strange things were happening. The brothers were now accused of stealing a silver cup. Their actions, they felt, had proven that they wouldn't do such a thing, and, in fact, they were right.

However, again, they did not understand what was happening, as they had not understood the entirety of this scenario. How could they?

Joseph, whom they knew as someone else, had been so kind to them, even inviting them to eat at his house and then restoring their brother Simeon. The atmosphere had been one of trust and kindness, and now this!

Why would he suddenly turn and accuse them of stealing something out of his house, which, to say the least, would be a very serious crime.

Knowing they had not done such a thing, they suggested that if the silver cup was found in any sack, the one to whom that sack belonged, his life would be forfeited, and all of them would become slaves of Joseph.

They were right, and they were wrong. They were right in that they didn't steal the cup, but they were wrong in that it was not in one of the sacks.

BENJAMIN'S SACK

"And he said, Now also let it be according unto your words: he with whom it is found shall be my servant: and you shall be blameless.

"Then they speedily took down every man his sack to the ground, and opened every man his sack.

"And he searched, and began at the eldest, and left at the youngest: and the cup was found in Benjamin's sack.

"Then they rent their clothes, and loaded every man his donkey, and returned to the city.

"And Judah and his brethren came to Joseph's house; for he was yet there: and they fell before him on the ground.

"And Joseph said unto them, What deed is this that you have done? do you not know that a man as I can certainly divine?" (Gen. 44:10-15).

The same steward who had greeted them previously now stood before them as it regarded the cup that was supposedly missing. He was the one who had placed the cup in Benjamin's sack, so he knew exactly where it was.

Knowing they had not taken the cup, they made brash statements concerning their situation. He took them partially at their word.

Only the one in whose sack the cup would be found would be punished. He would be a slave, and the others could go free.

The cup, of course, was found in Benjamin's sack.

JUDAH

Chapter 44 of Genesis contains one of the most impassioned pleas ever made by one man to another. Judah made this plea unto Joseph.

His plea was so graphic, so touching, and so sincere that I feel it would be profitable for us to print the entirety of what was said by Judah to Joseph as it concerned his father Jacob and his brother Benjamin. Of course, Judah had no inkling whatsoever that he was speaking with Joseph.

The Scripture says: *"And Judah said, What shall we say unto my lord? what shall we speak? or how shall we clear ourselves? God has found out the iniquity of your servants: behold, we are my lord's servants, both we, and he also with whom the cup is found.*

"And he (Joseph) *said, God forbid that I should do so: but the man in whose hand the cup is found, he shall be my servant; and as for you, get you up in peace unto your father.*

"*Then Judah came near unto him, and said, O my lord, let your servant, I pray you, speak a word in my lord's ears, and let not your anger burn against your servant: for you are even as Pharaoh.*

"*My lord asked his servants, saying, Have you a father, or a brother?*

"*And we said unto my lord, we have a father, an old man, and a child of his old age, a little one; and his brother is dead, and he alone is left of his mother, and his father loves him.*

"*And you said unto your servants, Bring him down unto me, that I may set my eyes upon him.*

"*And we said unto my lord, The lad cannot leave his father: for if he should leave his father, his father would die.*

"*And you said unto your servants, Except your youngest brother come down with you, you shall see my face no more.*

"*And it came to pass when we came up unto your servant my father, we told him the words of my lord.*

"*And our father said, Go again, and buy us a little food.*

"*And we said, We cannot go down: if our youngest brother be with us, then will we go down: for we may not see the man's face, except our youngest brother be with us.*

"*And your servant my father said unto us, You know that my wife bore me two sons:*

"*And the one went out from me, and I said, Surely he is torn in pieces; and I saw him not since:*

"*And if you take this also from me, and mischief befall him, you shall bring down my gray hairs with sorrow to the grave.*

"*Now therefore when I come to your servant my father, and the lad be not with us; seeing that his life is bound up in the lad's life;*

"*It shall come to pass, when he sees that the lad is not with us, that he will die: and your servants shall bring down the gray hairs of your servant our father with sorrow to the grave.*

"*For your servant became surety for the lad unto my father, saying, If I bring him not unto you, then I shall bear the blame to my father forever.*

"*Now therefore, I pray you, let your servant abide instead of the lad a bondman to my lord; and let the lad go up with his brethren.*

"*For how shall I go up to my father, and the lad be not with me? lest peradventure I see the evil that shall come on my father*" (Gen. 44:16-34).

ISRAEL ON A COMING GLAD DAY

As well, all of this portrays a future day. Zechariah 9:13 says, "*When I have bent Judah for Me.*" In that day, at the second coming of the Lord, Judah will repent.

Zechariah, as well, said, "*In that day shall there be a great mourning*" (Zech. 12:11).

Verse 18 of this chapter says, *"Then Judah came near unto him."* Finally, at the second coming, Judah will *come near unto Jesus.* Joseph's brethren had no concept of all that was to flow to them from their conduct toward him. *"They took him, and cast him into a pit ... And they sat down to eat bread"* (Gen. 37:24-25). The Prophet Amos said, *"Woe to them ... Who drink wine in bowls, and anoint themselves with the chief ointments: but they are not grieved for the affliction of Joseph"* (Amos 6:1, 6).

Then strange things began to happen. At first, they took the seven years of plenty in stride, but then the seven years of famine were worse than anything they had ever known. Little did these sons of Jacob — the brothers of Joseph — know or realize that, despite the fact that it was touching many nations and untold numbers of people, all of this was because of them.

Then on the first trip to Egypt, there were very strange things happening, which resulted in Simeon being left behind, actually held in prison, with the command given to them that unless they brought their younger brother Benjamin back with them, there was no need in coming.

JACOB

Jacob had been so chagrined at the thought of Benjamin leaving that he did not agree that it could be done until there was no alternative. Judah took responsibility, and now their worst fears had been realized. Benjamin had been accused of stealing a silver cup belonging to the lord of Egypt, and it was demanded by the lord of Egypt that Benjamin remain behind, in fact, taking Simeon's place in prison.

At this demand, Judah now came before Joseph, and he made the most impassioned plea that has probably ever been recorded.

All of this had brought them to the feet of the injured Joseph. How marked is the display of God's own hand in all of this! There they stood, with the arrow of conviction thrust through and through their consciences, in the very presence of the man whom they, with wicked hands, had cast into the pit. Surely their sin had found them out, but it was in the presence of Joseph. Blessed place!

HOW SHALL I GO TO MY FATHER, AND THE LAD BE NOT WITH ME?

Judah closed out his plea with the pathos of the others being felt, as well, by saying to Joseph, *"For how shall I go up to my father, and the lad be not with me?"*

The tests have finally come to an end. Joseph was fully satisfied that these men were not the same men who sold him into Egyptian bondage. We must realize that the entirety of this scenario, which affected all of the Middle East, was all brought about in order to further the great plan of God. Joseph, along with Jacob, would figure very prominently in all of this, but so would these brothers. They had to be what they ought to be, and Joseph was now satisfied that the miracle of transformation had definitely taken place. The distress of

Judah, and all the others for that matter, shows that they were no longer in heart the men of those years ago. They declared that they loved their father too much to be indifferent to his tears and their brother Benjamin to consent to his captivity.

"Days are filled with sorrow and care,
"Hearts are lonely and drear;
"Burdens are lifted at Calvary,
"Jesus is very near."

"Cast your care on Jesus today,
"Leave your worry and fear;
"Burdens are lifted at Calvary,
"Jesus is very near."

"Troubled soul, the Saviour can see,
"Every heartache and tear;
"Burdens are lifted at Calvary,
"Jesus is very near."

JOSEPH

CHAPTER

11

JOSEPH MAKES HIMSELF KNOWN

CHAPTER ELEVEN

JOSEPH MAKES HIMSELF KNOWN

"Then Joseph could not refrain himself before all them who stood by him; and he cried, Cause every man to go out from me. And there stood no man with him, while Joseph made himself known unto his brothers" (Gen. 45:1).

Without a doubt, this is one of the most memorable, touching scenes in history. Even above the drama of this happening, we know it portrays that glad morning when Christ will reveal Himself to Israel, which will take place immediately after the second coming (Zech. 12:10).

In the first place, only God could bring about such a happening. Joseph was a Hebrew boy just 17 years of age when he was sold into Egypt as a slave by his brothers. He was then placed in prison in Egypt because of false charges and then miraculously and instantly elevated to the second highest position in that land and, thereby, the world. As stated, only God could do such a thing.

JOSEPH'S REACTION

As Judah finished his impassioned plea, closing out with the words, *"For how shall I go up to my father, and the lad be not with me?"* Joseph could refrain himself no longer.

Suddenly, he stated to the Egyptians who were with him in the room that all should leave with the exception of his brothers and himself.

Once again, Joseph's reactions were strange. The brothers were still overly confused concerning the recent happenings about the silver cup. They knew that Benjamin was not guilty of taking the cup. The solemn tones of Joseph still rang in their ears as he said that the person in whose hand the cup was found must be his slave and, thereby, must remain in Egypt. They knew that if this happened, it would kill Jacob. Then Judah, sick at heart, made his impassioned plea to Joseph and, first of all, referred to their terrible sin of selling Joseph into Egypt some 22 years before.

Not knowing what to expect and burdened down with sorrow, the room must have been deathly quiet as the Egyptian guards and attendants left as commanded by Joseph.

WEEPING

"And he wept aloud: and the Egyptians and the house of Pharaoh heard" (Gen. 45:2).

Without warning, Joseph broke into loud sobs and weeping. As stated, he could refrain himself no longer. As well, he didn't want the Egyptians who were present to hear what he would have to say as it regarded the sin of these men. Joseph's grace in covering up their sin as soon as they confessed it, hiding it from Pharaoh, and hasting to acknowledge them before Pharaoh as his brothers illustrates the richer grace of Him who says: *"Your sins and iniquities will I remember no more."*

No stranger is allowed to witness this sacred scene. In fact, what stranger could understand or appreciate it? We are called here to witness, as it were, divinely-wrought conviction in the presence of divine grace. As well, we may say that when these two, conviction and grace, come together, such always presents a settlement of every question.

The reader must understand these words because they are very, very important! The problems may be many. The difficulties, in whatever realm, may be insurmountable or even impossible as it regards man. However, if Holy Spirit conviction is responded to properly by the individual, the grace of God will always and without exception be made evident in such a case, which guarantees the solution of every problem.

ONLY GOD ...

Only God can do this, and to bring it to pass, it merely requires faith, surrender, and obedience on the part of the individual. If man attempts (which he always does) to ameliorate a situation by other means, he — able to deal with the externals only — can effect no real change. However, Holy Spirit conviction weighing heavily on the heart deals with the real problem and its cause. To be sure, in some way, the cause is always rebellion against God and God's way. Sin is not so much the act, although it is that, as it is rebellion. It's man attempting to function by his own means and machinations, which always leads to wreckage. God's way is *"Jesus Christ and Him crucified"* (I Cor. 1:23; 2:2; Gal. 6:14; Eph. 2:13-18; Col. 2:14-15).

Joseph wept so loudly that the Egyptians, who had just left the room, could not help but overhear his loud sobbing.

"The house of Pharaoh hearing," means that the officials who had previously been in the room reported the happenings to Pharaoh.

I AM JOSEPH

"And Joseph said unto his brothers, I am Joseph; does my father yet live? And his brothers could not answer him; for they were troubled at his presence" (Gen. 45:3).

Concerning this moment, Pulpit Commentary says, *"The effect of this announcement can be better imagined than described. Hitherto he had been known to his brethren as Zaphnath-paaneah."*

At the sound of this name, and the fact that Joseph himself said it and, no doubt, spoke to them in Hebrew, it would have filled them with consternation. Perhaps this is the reason that Joseph, discerning their countenances, asked so abruptly about Jacob, especially considering that a short time before they had mentioned that Jacob was well (Gen. 43:27-28).

The simple statement, *"I am Joseph,"* explained all the strange happenings, but yet, they could hardly believe their ears.

How in the world could their brother, whom they sold into Egyptian bondage, now be the governor of all of Egypt and, thereby, the second most powerful man in the world? How could such a thing have happened?

EGYPT

"And Joseph said unto his brothers, Come near to me, I pray you. And they came near. And he said, I am Joseph your brother, whom you sold into Egypt" (Gen. 45:4).

The text indicates that they didn't know what to do. They were transfixed to the spot where they were standing, not knowing what to say, what to do, or how to act.

Joseph mentioned quietly that they should now come closer to him, which they did. So as to make sure they understood exactly what he had said, he amplified the statement by saying, *"I am Joseph your brother, whom you sold into Egypt."*

Quite possibly, he wondered if they understood when he first said, *"I am Joseph."* So now, he identified himself in such a way that there could be no misunderstanding. He was the brother who was sold as a slave.

A GREAT DELIVERANCE

"Now therefore be not grieved, nor angry with your-selves, that you sold me hither: for God did send me before you to preserve life.

"For these two years has the famine been in the land: and yet there are five years, in the which there shall neither be earing nor harvest.

"And God sent me before you to preserve you a posterity in the earth, and to save your lives by a great deliverance" (Gen. 45:5-7).

Joseph's heart beat true to God and to his brothers. He kept pressing upon them that it was God who had taken him out of the pit and placed him upon the throne.

The way he said all of this led them to feel and to know that it was against God that they had sinned rather than against himself, which actually was true and made the sin even worse. And yet, he assured them that God loved them and overruled all for their salvation, as He will do for anyone who comes to Him in humble repentance.

Joseph attempted to lessen their grief and sorrow by show-ing them that whatever it was they intended, God overruled it and turned it around for good, as only He can do.

We must all grieve over our failures, for such must never be taken lightly. However, God can take that which is degrading, even gross sin as the brothers of Joseph, and bring good out of it, with no thanks to the sinner, as would be obvious.

We should look carefully at how Joseph responded to his brothers. He constantly dwelt on how God had turned this thing around, because it was true. However, at the same time, it served as encouragement for his brothers, even as it was meant to do. This is very important!

Dealing with those who have failed but have truly repented should be handled exactly as Joseph handled this situation. However, the great question is, *"If placed in Joseph's shoes and in his time, how many Christians would have conducted themselves exactly as Joseph did?"*

I'm afraid that many would have taken the opportunity to exact their pound of flesh. Such, as would be obvious, is certainly not Christlike and, in fact, puts the wronged person in the position of committing sin by acting in that manner.

TELL MY FATHER JACOB ...

"So now it was not you who sent me hither, but God: and He has made me a father to Pharaoh, and lord of all his house, and a ruler throughout all the land of Egypt.

"Make haste, and go up to my father, and say unto him, Thus says your son Joseph, God has made me lord of all Egypt: come down unto me, tarry not:

"And you shall dwell in the land of Goshen, and you shall be near unto me, you, and your children, and your children's children, and your flocks, and your herds, and all that you have:

"And there will I nourish you; for yet there are five years of famine; lest you, and your household, and all that you have, come to poverty.

"And, behold, your eyes see, and the eyes of my brother Benjamin, that it is my mouth that speaks unto you.

"And you shall tell my father of all my glory in Egypt, and of all that you have seen; and you shall haste and bring down my father hither" (Gen. 45:8-13).

Now, Joseph gave instructions as to his father Jacob, but the brothers had another problem with that:

They were going to have to confess to Jacob what had happened with Joseph those 22 years before. Even though the news was going to be wonderful and glorious, because of their culpability and having to confess to Jacob what actually happened, it would have a bittersweet effect.

THE PLANS OF GOD

Joseph was telling his father that he must come down to Egypt. As we shall see, even though his beloved son Joseph said this, the great patriarch would have to hear from the Lord before he would consent to make the move. However, he would hear from Jehovah, and the command would be even more emphatic regarding his transfer to Egypt.

Once again, the plans of God were much larger than anything we could ever begin to think. While Egypt would be very good to Jacob, it would not prove to be so good to those who would follow after, for the children of Israel would remain in Egypt for some 215 years before being delivered by the mighty power of God.

They would fall from the lofty station of place and position down to the far lower level of slavery. Still, there were plusses in all of this, as well, with one of them guaranteeing that, for the most part, Israel would remain to themselves and not intermarry with the Egyptians.

Verse 13 speaks of Joseph telling his brothers to tell Jacob of *"all my glory in Egypt."* The Prophet Isaiah said: *"And they shall declare My glory among the Gentiles"* (Isa. 66:19). Thus will the glory of Christ be made manifest in that coming day.

REUNION

"And he fell upon his brother Benjamin's neck, and wept; and Benjamin wept upon his neck.

"Moreover he kissed all his brothers, and wept upon them: and after that his brothers talked with him.

"And the fame thereof was heard in Pharaoh's house, saying, Joseph's brothers are come: and it pleased Pharaoh well, and his servants" (Gen. 45:14-16).

This had to be extremely traumatic for Benjamin as well. He was born after Joseph was sold into Egypt, so he had never seen his brother. At some point in time, he was, no doubt, told the story that his father Jacob had been told, that Joseph had died as the result of wild beasts. The brothers would not have dared to tell him that they had sold Joseph as a slave into Egypt.

Whether the correct information was given to him immediately, the brothers told him on the way home, or they waited until they told it to their father Jacob, we aren't told. At any rate, Joseph is alive!

Joseph kissing all of his brothers portrays the seal of recognition, of reconciliation, and of salvation.

Concerning this scene, the Pulpit Commentary says, *"It has been thought that Benjamin stood when Joseph embraced him, and that the two wept upon each other's neck, but that the brethren bowed themselves at Joseph's feet, causing the expression to be, 'and he wept upon them.'"*

More than likely, that's exactly the way it happened. His kissing them, in effect, stated that the past was done, and it must not mar the future.

It had taken 22 years and much suffering along the way to come to this place, but patience had now been rewarded. In fact, trust in God is never unrewarded.

Joseph allowed the Spirit of God to work out this thing and did not try to insert his own efforts, as we all are so prone to do. When the Lord does it, it is done well! In the main, trust in the Lord never brings anything but good news.

PHARAOH

"And Pharaoh said unto Joseph, Say unto your brothers, This do you; load your beasts, and go, and get you unto the land of Canaan;

*"And take your father and your households, and come
unto me: and I will give you the good of the land of Egypt,
and you shall eat the fat of the land.*

*"Now you are commanded, this do you; take you wag-
ons out of the land of Egypt for your little ones, and for your
wives, and bring your father, and come.*

*"Also regard not your stuff; for the good of all the land of
Egypt is yours"* (Gen. 45:17-20).

It had been told Pharaoh that the brothers of Joseph had
come, but, of course, Pharaoh knew nothing about the situation at hand.

The monarch evidently called Joseph before him and gave
him special permission to bring his entire family into the land
of Egypt. Every evidence is that he did this gladly.

In fact, they were to be given land in the area of Goshen,
all at the expense of the state.

Pharaoh informed Joseph that he wished so much to lavish
good things upon Joseph's family that he told them not to even
bother to bring their *"stuff"* from Canaan because everything
that would be needed would be provided in Egypt. This, in
effect, was a carte blanche proposal.

Pharaoh was very quick and very glad to do this simply
because Joseph had been the saviour of Egypt. As it was, they
had plenty of grain stored up to last out the famine and, as
well, to sell grain to surrounding nations. Had it not been for
Joseph, Egypt would now be in dire straits exactly as these
other countries now were. So Pharaoh gladly provided this
which Joseph's family would need.

THE CHILDREN OF ISRAEL

"And the children of Israel did so: and Joseph gave them wagons, according to the commandment of Pharaoh, and gave them provision for the way.

"To all of them he gave each man changes of raiment; but to Benjamin he gave three hundred pieces of silver, and five changes of raiment.

"And to his father he sent after this manner; ten donkeys loaded with the good things of Egypt, and ten she donkeys loaded with corn and bread and meat for his father by the way.

"So he sent his brothers away, and they departed: and he said unto them, See that you fall not out by the way" (Gen. 45:21-24).

When the brethren of Joseph left this time, they were not fearful that some untoward thing would happen to them as it had before. Now they understood the reason for the strange events that took place on the first trip and the first part of this last trip.

They were going back to Canaan with wagons sent for the very purpose of bringing all the goods of Jacob and the entirety of the families back to Egypt. So, there must have been quite a number of wagons.

As well, they were given beautiful changes of clothing, with Benjamin being given 300 pieces of silver as well. Think of the difference of what they had done to Joseph those 22 years earlier.

They had taken his coat of many colors, stained it with the blood of a kid of the goats, and had sent it by the hand of a slave to convince Jacob that Joseph had been killed. As well, they had sold Joseph into Egypt for 20 pieces of silver.

However, the raiment that Joseph gave them was beautiful beyond compare, in fact, such as they had never had in their lives and never hoped to have. What an expression of love!

It is the same with Christ, for Joseph was a type of Christ. The old song says:

"I traded my sins for salvation,
"I traded my load for relief.
"What I got was so much more
"Than what He received,
"I sure got the best of the trade."

When you put the two scenes together, you are then seeing what we have done to Christ and then in turn, what He has done for us.

There is no way that one can properly grasp the fullness of the love of Christ. What He has done for us, and for which He paid such a great price on the Cross, will stand good forever and forever.

"Christ our Redeemer died on the Cross,
"Died for the sinner, paid all his due;
"Sprinkle your soul with the blood of the Lamb,
"And I will pass, will pass over you."

"Chiefest of sinners, Jesus will save;
"All He has promised, that will He do;
"Wash in the fountain opened for sin,
"And I will pass, will pass over you."

"Judgment is coming, all will be there,
"Each one receiving justly his due;
"Hide in the saving, sin cleansing blood,
"And I will pass, will pass over you."

"Oh great compassion; Oh boundless love
"Oh loving kindness, faithful and true!
"Find peace and shelter under the blood,
"And I will pass, will pass over you."

JOSEPH

CHAPTER

12

THE MEETING

CHAPTER TWELVE

THE MEETING

"And Joseph made ready his chariot, and went up to meet Israel his father, to Goshen, and presented himself unto him; and he fell on his neck, and wept on his neck a good while" (Gen. 46:29).

Joseph making ready his chariot and going up to meet his father tells us very little in the translation; however, in the Hebrew, such terminology is commonly used of the appearance of God or His angels. It is employed here in this manner to indicate the glory in which Joseph came to meet Jacob.

In Verse 29 just quoted, the Holy Spirit referred to the patriarch as *Israel* as he met Joseph for the first time in more than 20 years. Among other things, the Holy Spirit referred to him as Israel because of the future meeting that will take place when Israel and the Lord Jesus Christ meet at the second coming after such a long estrangement.

Joseph's chariot was of the royal house and was probably unlike anything that Jacob had ever seen. It would have been pulled by the finest and the most beautiful horses. As well, with Joseph, there were probably many attendants and guards who were also riding in gilded chariots and dressed in the finery of Egypt. After all, we must remember that Joseph was second only to Pharaoh, and with Egypt possibly being the greatest nation in the world, it meant that Joseph was the second most powerful man in the world at that time.

KING OF KINGS AND LORD OF LORDS

Also, Joseph didn't do this solely for his father, but this was actually the manner in which this prime minister traveled, which served to exhibit his authority.

In all of this, there was a greater spiritual meaning. When Jesus came the first time, He, in fact, came as a humble peasant. Israel knew Him as the carpenter's son, which means that He definitely was not of the Jewish aristocracy. However, when He comes the second time, He will not come as a peasant, but rather as King of kings and Lord of lords. In fact, as it refers to splendor and glory, there is absolutely nothing that can even remotely compare with that which will accompany Christ when He comes back to this Earth.

So, when Israel sees Him at that time and accepts Him as Lord and Saviour, it will be in a glory that beggars all description. In fact, the very planetary bodies of the heavens will dance in glee, so to speak, when our Lord shall come back to Earth again (Mat. 24:29-30). The Creator has now come back to His creation, and we speak of planet

Earth, where He will ultimately make His eternal headquarters (Rev., Chpts. 21-22). So, the meeting of Joseph with his father Jacob is meant to portray that coming day, hence, the glory that accompanied Joseph.

The evidence is that Jacob and all of his entourage went first of all to the area called Goshen. It would have been in the area very close to modern Cairo.

How long Jacob had been settled there before Joseph came, we aren't told; however, it could not have been very long, probably only a few days.

JOSEPH IS COMING

When they informed Jacob that Joseph was coming, I wonder what the thoughts were of the great patriarch. He had never hoped to see Joseph again, and it had been over 20 years since he had laid eyes on him. In fact, Joseph was only 17 years old when he last saw him. He was now about 38 or 39.

When Joseph came into the presence of Jacob, he fell on his neck, which means that he embraced him grandly, with him weeping as, no doubt, Jacob did as well. However, this time, it was tears of joy. Faith had now been honored as heartache of the past 20 and more years had been wiped away. It was now only a dim memory; Joseph was here, and Joseph was yet alive!

Strangely and beautifully enough, this is the story of Israel. Prophetically speaking, the meeting that we are describing here is yet to take place; however, it is closer now than ever. The seven years of dark trouble, typified by the seven years of famine, are yet to come to Israel, but come they shall. At the end of those seven years of terrible trouble (called *Jacob's trouble*), Jesus Christ is coming back and will, in fact, be the Saviour of Israel just as Joseph was the saviour of Israel.

ISRAEL

"And Israel said unto Joseph, Now let me die, since I have seen your face, because you are yet alive" (Gen. 46:30).

Without a doubt, this was the happiest moment of Jacob's life, and no wonder! That which he never dreamed would happen had, miracle of miracles, come true.

In the patriarch's mind, his life's journey had now filled its course. The last earthly longing of his heart had been completely satisfied. Whenever God willed, he was now ready to be gathered to his fathers.

However, the Lord would see fit to allow this great man to live another 17 years and to enjoy the fullest of the blessings of God. The Lord had asked Jacob to go through a great sorrow, so great, in fact, that it defies description, but He would now make up for that sorrow, and do so manifold. The Lord will never owe any man anything.

The truth is, the Lord has never owed anyone anything; however, even if He asks us to do something that is difficult, He, without fail, will always reimburse us, and will do so exactly as He did with Jacob.

Not counting the five grandsons of Joseph, there would have been 70 people there that day when Joseph met Jacob.

This number included all of the children. What questions the children must have had! Could they understand that Joseph was the lord of Egypt, and yet, the son of Jacob and, in essence, their uncle?

The number 70 became afterwards a symbolic number among the Israelites — as in the 70 elders of Moses, the 70 of the Sanhedrin, the 70 disciples of the Lord, etc.

There may be something in the combination of numbers. Seventy is seven times 10. Ten is the Biblical symbol of the complete development of humanity, seven of perfection. Therefore, 70 may symbolize the elect people of God as the hope of humanity — Israel in Egypt.

In the 12 patriarchs and the 70 souls, we certainly see the foreshadowing of the Saviour's appointments in the beginning of the Christian church. The small number of Israel in the midst of the great multitude of Egypt is a great encouragement to faith. *"Who has despised the day of small things?"*

SHEPHERDS

"And Joseph said unto his brethren, and unto his father's house, I will go up, and show Pharaoh, and say unto him, My brethren, and my father's house, which were in the land of Canaan, are come unto me;

"And the men are shepherds, for their trade has been to feed cattle; and they have brought their flocks, and their herds, and all that they have.

"And it shall come to pass, when Pharaoh shall call you, and shall say, What is your occupation?

"That you shall say, Your servants' trade has been about cattle from our youth even until now, both we, and also our fathers: that you may dwell in the land of Goshen; for every shepherd is an abomination unto the Egyptians" (Gen. 46:31-34).

Goshen seemed to be the most fertile part of Egypt, at least as it referred to the grazing of cattle and sheep. The Nile River ran through this area, and it finally settled into the marshlands of the Nile Delta, which afforded it much grass.

While flocks of cattle and herds of sheep were held by the Egyptians and even by Pharaoh, those who attended these flocks and herds were looked down on by the Egyptians. As well, the word *abomination* used in Verse 34, as it regarded shepherds, meant that there was some religious connotation to the attitude of the Egyptians toward the shepherds.

At any rate, Joseph did not attempt to conceal from Pharaoh the low caste of the shepherds, his brothers, but he trusted in God that what was an abomination to the Egyptians would by the grace of God be made acceptable.

As well, if they kept to themselves in Goshen, the Israelites were not likely to intermingle with the Egyptians and, thereby, intermarry.

Egypt was an agricultural nation, which meant that her population was made up of farmers, as much as they despised herdsman. Their monuments picture shepherds as distorted, dirty, and emaciated figures.

"Washed in the blood, by the Spirit sealed,
"Christ in His Word is to me revealed;
"Glory to God! And my soul does shine,
"God my salvation, and His life is mine!"

"Once I was blind, but behold I see;
"God from above now has shined unto me;
"Cleansed from all sin, in His Word I behold,
"Wealth which can never be compared to gold."

"O that the world might the Saviour see,
"That blessed Saviour who saved poor me!
"O how the lost ones would come shouting home,
"Never, never, never, nevermore to roam!"

"Washed in the blood! Sinner come today;
"Jesus so freely the debt will pay;
"Come to His arms, to His arms of grace,
"Come, now in meekness, seek the Saviour's face."

JOSEPH

CHAPTER

13

PHARAOH

CHAPTER THIRTEEN

PHARAOH

"Then Joseph came and told Pharaoh, and said, My father and my brethren, and their flocks, and their herds, and all that they have, are come out of the land of Canaan; and, behold, they are in the land of Goshen.

"And he took some of his brethren, even five men, and presented them unto Pharaoh" (Gen. 47:1-2).

As far as we know, no one in Egypt ever knew anything about the wickedness of the past deeds of Joseph's brothers. Such is true forgiveness. It not only forgives sin, but it forgets as well.

Though Joseph was a great man, and despite the fact that his brothers were shepherds, which means that the Egyptians despised such, yet he openly owned them. Despite what we were, our Lord Jesus is not ashamed to call us brethren. The brothers being shepherds, which Joseph had been, as well, served as a type of the Good Shepherd who would someday come and, in fact, did!

In this appearance of Joseph before Pharaoh, it seems that he went in first and told Pharaoh that his father and brethren with all their flocks were now in the land of Goshen.

He then brought in five of his brothers and presented them to Pharaoh, and last of all, he *"brought in Jacob his father, and set him before Pharaoh."*

Joseph wanted his family in Goshen, for that was the best place for pasture. In fact, they were there now, but Joseph must observe protocol and ask permission from Pharaoh before everything could be settled, which he did.

THE SAVIOUR OF EGYPT

Of course, there was no way that Pharaoh would refuse Joseph. In fact, Joseph, as was overly obvious, was the saviour of Egypt. Due to the provisions made by Joseph, Egypt, in effect, was now the saviour of the world of the Middle East. No nation in the area of the famine had any sustenance except Egypt. This was because of Joseph and, in reality, because of the Lord. Pharaoh owed everything to Joseph, so his request was met with instant approval.

Joseph taking five of his brothers in to see Pharaoh after he had the first conference portrays the fact that his request had been granted, which, of course, I'm sure he knew that it would.

Why he took only five of his brothers is interesting. Why not take all of them? Quite possibly, five was a very special number to the Egyptians, even as seven later became to Israel.

GOSHEN

"And Pharaoh said unto his brethren, What is your occupation? And they said unto Pharaoh, Your servants are shepherds, both we, and also our fathers.

"They said moreover unto Pharaoh, For to sojourn in the land are we come; for your servants have no pasture for their flocks; for the famine is sore in the land of Canaan: now therefore, we pray you, let your servants dwell in the land of Goshen.

"And Pharaoh spoke unto Joseph, saying, Your father and your brethren are come unto you:

"The land of Egypt is before you; in the best of the land make your father and brethren to dwell; in the land of Goshen let them dwell: and if you know any men of activity among them, then make them rulers over my cattle" (Gen. 47:3-6).

Occupations were hereditary among the Egyptians, and thus, the five brothers answered Pharaoh that they were shepherds and that their father and grandfather had been such before them. Consequently, Pharaoh would conclude that in their case, no change was possible or desired in their mode of life.

They asked for permission to dwell in the land of Goshen, even though Joseph had already received such permission. They were, as well, merely following protocol.

Pharaoh answered in a bountiful way, telling them that *"the land of Egypt was before them,"* and that they could have anything they desired. However, if it was Goshen that they desired, then that's what they would have.

He further added that if desired, Joseph could give his brothers employment as being over the vast herds of Pharaoh. In other words, they would be working for the state, which, more than likely, they did, and which these jobs would have been excellent promotions in their case. In other words, they were well taken care of regarding finances.

JACOB

"And Joseph brought in Jacob his father, and set him before Pharaoh: and Jacob blessed Pharaoh" (Gen. 47:7).

Going back to several months previously, the moment when Joseph revealed himself in his glory to his brethren was when Judah took the sorrow of the aged Israel to heart and put himself into it. It is a wonderful picture of Christ's revelation of Himself when Judah in the latter day will voice the sorrow of Israel in connection with the rejection of Jesus, the true Joseph.

Joseph was not ashamed of his brethren. He presented them to the great king. Jacob, although he had to confess a short and troubled life and was himself a despised shepherd, yet blessed the mighty monarch; *"and without contradiction, the less is blessed of the greater."*

All of this means that the least and most faltering of God's children is superior to the mightiest monarch and is conscious of the superiority.

In the story of Joseph, we have had a series of meetings that have been astounding in their presentation and far-reaching in their consequences. After bringing in his five brothers to Pharaoh, last of all he brought in his father Jacob.

What must have Jacob thought when as a lowly shepherd, he walked into what must have been one of the grandest buildings, if not the grandest, on the face of the earth, the palace of Pharaoh, head of the mightiest nation of the world of that day? This is a setting that Jacob in his wildest dreams could never have imagined, but yet, it quickly became obvious that despite the glory and the splendor of this palatial empire, Jacob was the better. Pharaoh knew that as well.

SUPERIORITY

Pharaoh, no doubt, imagined that the tremendous powers possessed by Joseph, which were unequaled anywhere in the world of that day, had to have had their seedbed in the life of this aged patriarch who stood before them, and he was right. As Pharaoh looked at this aged man, little did he realize, but yet sensed, that a power greater than anything he knew resided in the heart of this frail patriarch. As he looked at Jacob, this heathen never dreamed that the man standing before him would be thought of throughout eternal ages as the third one in the great appellative, *"the God of Abraham, Isaac, and Jacob."*

Knowing the protocol of the time, it would have to be that Pharaoh, despite the splendor and glory of his surroundings, and despite the frailty of this aged man, requested that Jacob bless him. As stated, *"the less is blessed of the better."*

As Jacob reached out and laid his gnarled, aged hand on the head of Pharaoh and proceeded to bless him, such typified the coming glad day when Israel, with Jesus standing by her side, will bless the Gentile world. It will happen at the beginning of the great millennial reign and will last throughout that definite time.

PHARAOH

"And Pharaoh said unto Jacob, How old are you?

"And Jacob said unto Pharaoh, The days of the years of my pilgrimage are an hundred and thirty years: few and evil have the days of the years of my life been, and have not attained unto the days of the years of the life of my fathers in the days of their pilgrimage.

"And Jacob blessed Pharaoh, and went out from before Pharaoh" (Gen. 47:8-10).

This was a first for Egypt, for never before had such a prayer been heard within an Egyptian palace. Still, we must believe that the conduct of Pharaoh was mostly due to the effect of Joseph's life and ministry. One true man is a great power in any country.

Jacob, being 130 years old at that time, was evidently much older than most, if not all, of the people in Egypt as it regarded longevity. I think the facts are, at least during this particular period of time, that as a whole, those who served the Lord lived much longer than their contemporaries in the heathen world.

I think this was true then in Egypt, and I think it was true in all other countries as well.

From the text, it seems that Pharaoh knew that Jacob was very aged just by looking at him; consequently, he asked him his age with Jacob replying that he was 130. I doubt seriously that there was anyone in Egypt at that time who was 100 years old, much less the age of Jacob.

But yet, as Jacob confessed, he was not as old as his fathers. In fact, he would die at 147 years of age, some 17 years after coming into Egypt. His grandfather Abraham died at 175 and his father Isaac at 180.

JOSEPH, THE GREAT BENEFACTOR

Joseph, raised from the pit to the throne, a type of Christ, enriched his brethren with all the promises that they, by their rejection of him, had forfeited, but they were now restored to them upon the ground of grace. They were given the richest province in Egypt.

The Egyptians themselves, representative of all the nations of the earth, were saved from death by Joseph and made by him the willing slaves of the throne with their future assured to them. All of this is a striking picture of what has yet to come to pass, but most definitely shall!

Actually, this is the subject of Romans, Chapters 9, 10, and 11, in which it is pointed out that Israel and the Gentile will inherit the promises in fellowship solely upon the ground of pure grace.

Joseph was the greatest benefactor Egypt ever had. In one day by divine wisdom, he destroyed slavery and land-lordism. He set up only one master and one landlord in the nation, and that was the nation itself, as physically embodied in Pharaoh.

THE SEVEN YEARS OF FAMINE

From this account, we learn just how severe the famine actually was. Had it not been for Joseph, no doubt, hundreds of thousands, if not millions, would have died of starvation. However, because of the divine wisdom given to him, he was able to forecast the famine and lay in store for that coming time. Then, again by divine wisdom, he was able to nourish the people as the famine became more and more severe.

The people seemed to have done fairly well in the first year of the famine and possibly even the second year, but by the time of the third year, the situation had become critical and remained that way, even growing steadily worse to the conclusion of this terrible seven-year period.

When Joseph levied the 20 percent tax, this was one of the fairest arrangements that any people had ever known. Undoubtedly, it was the Lord who gave him this wisdom. In fact, it is seldom equaled in any country presently. For instance, at this particular time (2014), counting state, local, and federal income taxes, it approximates 50 percent in the United States.

DIVINE WISDOM

Some have claimed that Joseph robbed the Egyptians of their liberties and converted a free people into a hoard of abject slaves. Nothing could be further from the truth.

In fact, had it not been for Joseph and the divine wisdom that he was given during this extremely trying time, as stated, millions of people would literally have starved to death. As it was, the people were looked after, and there is no record that anyone starved.

As well, when the famine ended and crops could be grown once again with the assurance of a bountiful harvest, Joseph allowed all the people to go back to their original land plots. He even gave them seed, equipment, and animals to work the land, with Pharaoh only getting 20 percent. To be frank and as stated, that was and is an excellent arrangement.

ISRAEL

"And Israel dwelt in the land of Egypt, in the country of Goshen; and they had possessions therein, and grew, and multiplied exceedingly" (Gen. 47:27).

In Verse 27, the nation is called *Israel* for the first time.

Feeble as was his body and imperfect as was his faith (as all faith on both counts is imperfect), yet did Jacob esteem God's land, the land of Canaan, and the promises connected therewith as unspeakably superior to Egypt with all its glory!

As we shall see, he made Joseph swear that when he died, he would put his bones where his heart was, in the land of Canaan.

The children of Israel came into Egypt 70 strong and would leave out about 215 years later with upwards of 3 million people.

Horton says: *"This is a summary verse letting us know that though Israel's family came to Egypt intending to stay temporarily, they continued to live in Goshen and settled down to stay. They were prosperous and kept increasing in number."*

After the death of Joseph, there would come a day that a Pharaoh would occupy the throne who held no affection for Joseph or the Hebrews; consequently, he would make slaves of them.

However, had that not been done, Israel would have had no desire whatsoever to leave Egypt and, in fact, would not have left. The Lord has to allow many things that are negative to come our way in order for us to desire to do His will.

CANAANLAND

"And Jacob lived in the land of Egypt seventeen years: so the whole age of Jacob was an hundred forty and seven years.

"And the time drew near that Israel must die: and he called his son Joseph, and said unto him, If now I have found grace in your sight, put, I pray you, your hand under my thigh, and deal kindly and truly with me; bury me not, I pray you, in Egypt:

"But I will lie with my fathers, and you shall carry me out of Egypt, and bury me in their buryingplace. And he said, I will do as you have said.

"And he said, Swear unto me. And he swore unto him. And Israel bowed himself upon the bed's head" (Gen. 47:28-31).

As previously stated, Jacob lived some 17 years in Egypt after arriving in that land, dying at 147 years old. However, he had brought about the sons who would make up the great tribes of Israel that would ultimately give the world the Word of God and, as well, serve as the womb of the Messiah. They were also meant to evangelize the world and, in effect, accomplished that through the Apostle Paul, even though Israel as a nation hated Paul.

To be sure, in the coming kingdom age, they will then gloriously fulfill that role. Of course, it will be done only after they accept Christ as their Saviour, their Lord, and their Messiah, which they will do at the second coming.

Jacob's life had been lived in the following places: Born in Canaan, he had lived 77 years in that land and then 20 years in Padan-aram. He then lived 33 years in Canaan again and now 17 in Egypt, 147 years in all.

THE PREDICTIONS

Now the great patriarch came down to die, but first, he would gloriously predict the future of his sons, or rather the tribes over which they would serve as the head.

THE AGED PATRIARCH

Mackintosh has a beautiful statement concerning Jacob's last days. He said:

"The close of Jacob's career stands in most pleasing contrast with all the previous scenes of his eventful history. It reminds one of a serene evening after a tempestuous day: The sun, which during the day had been hidden from view by clouds, mists, and fogs, sets in majesty and brightness, gilding with its beams the western sky, and holding out the cheering prospect of a bright tomorrow. Thus it is with our aged patriarch. The supplanting, the bargain-making, the cunning, the management, the shifting, the shuffling, the unbelieving selfish fears, all those dark clouds of nature and of earth seem to have passed away, and he comes forth in all the calm elevation of faith, to bestow blessings and impart dignities, in that holy skillfulness which communion with God can alone impact."

HIS HEART WAS IN CANAAN

Jacob realized, and graphically so, that God had blessed him exceedingly. The son he never hoped to see again now stood by his side. Not only that, his son was the prime minister of the greatest nation on earth. Along with that, the entirety of his family had been given the choicest part of Egypt in which to dwell and to pasture their flocks. As well, for some 17 years, he had lived a life of serenity, peace, and blessing, all coupled with the presence of the Lord.

However, as wonderful as all of that was, Egypt with all its glory was not his home. His heart was in Canaanland, that Promised Land which God promised to his grandfather Abraham when He called him out of Ur of the Chaldees, and then promised his father Isaac. The promise had been just as clear to him as well.

So, he made Joseph promise, even swear, that he would not bury him in Egypt, but that he would put his remains where his heart was — in the land of Canaan, which would one day be called *Israel*.

Verse 29 refers to Jacob as Israel because his faith shined brightly. He faced the prospect of death with his faith in the promise. It was so real and so outstanding to the patriarch that he even had Joseph put his hand under his thigh, the pro-creative part of man, signifying that a birth would take place in that land of promise exactly as the Lord had stated. When Joseph did as his father demanded, promising that he would carry him out of Egypt and bury him in the burying place of his grandfather Abraham and his father Isaac, the Scripture says that Jacob, i.e., Israel, bowed down on the head of his bed in praise and worship, which indicates that he was now satisfied.

Hebrews 11:21 says Jacob *"worshipped, leaning upon the top of his staff,"* but there is no contradiction. These are two different incidents.

Jacob's feelings concerning Egypt and the Promised Land should be our feelings, as well, as it regards this world and the portals of Glory. Even though this present world can have some attractions just as Egypt did for Jacob and his family, we must understand that this present world is not our abode. Our future is not here but rather with the Lord of Glory. No matter its present attractions, there is a *better country* awaiting us on the other side. We must live our lives accordingly with our roots in the promises of God rather than in this fleeting world.

> *"I will sing of my Redeemer,*
> *"And His wondrous love to me;*
> *"On the cruel Cross He suffered,*
> *"From the curse to set me free."*

> *"I will tell the wondrous story,*
> *"How my lost estate to save,*
> *"In His boundless love and mercy,*
> *"He the ransom freely gave."*

> *"I will praise my dear Redeemer,*
> *"His triumphant power I'll tell,*
> *"How the victory He giveth*
> *"Over sin, and death, and Hell."*

> *"I will sing of my Redeemer,*
> *"And His heavenly love to me;*
> *"He from death to life has brought me,*
> *"Son of God, with Him to be."*

JOSEPH

JOSEPH AND JACOB

JOSEPH AND JACOB

"And it came to pass after these things, that one told Joseph, Behold, your father is sick: and he took with him his two sons, Manasseh and Ephraim.

"And one told Jacob, and said, Behold, your son Joseph comes unto you: and Israel strengthened himself, and sat upon the bed" (Gen. 48:1-2).

When Joseph was informed that his father Jacob was ill, he hastened to go to his side, knowing that the old man didn't have a long time left. However, the Spirit of the Lord impressed Joseph to take his two sons, Manasseh and Ephraim, with him. In fact, great spiritual consequences would be involved. The boys must have been about 18 or 20 years old at the time.

Joseph wanted his two sons to know and realize that even though they had been born in Egypt, and all they had ever known was Egypt, still, they weren't Egyptians, but rather of the house of Jacob, i.e., "Israelites."

Such is a portrayal of believers who are born in this present world but, nevertheless, are not of this world, but rather of the world to come.

Finally, the significance of the change of name from Jacob to Israel is not to be overlooked. By faith (it is always faith) the great patriarch, moved upon by the Lord, would claim the promises and chart the course of Israel. Though the eyes of the patriarch were very dim in the natural, even as we shall see, his faith burned brightly, actually, brighter than ever, hence, he was called *Israel.*

GOD ALMIGHTY

"And Jacob said unto Joseph, God Almighty appeared unto me at Luz in the land of Canaan, and blessed me,

"And said unto me, Behold, I will make you fruitful, and multiply you, and I will make of you a multitude of people; and will give this land to your seed after you for an everlasting possession" (Gen. 48:3-4).

Jacob referred to God as *El Shaddai,* using the same name that God had used of Himself when He appeared to the patriarch at Beth-el, which was after the sad experience of Shechem (Gen. 35:7-15).

Along with relating this glorious experience, Jacob would also bring the promise in view. First of all, he proclaimed to Joseph that even though the promises of God may seem to be so grand and glorious that they are beyond our reach, God, in fact, will provide, and every single promise will be fulfilled.

As well, the promise of which he spoke was not material blessings, for Joseph already had that, and so did his sons and Jacob as well. He was looking beyond all of that to something of far greater magnitude. He was looking toward the purpose and reason for which this family had been raised up, brought from the loins of Abraham and the womb of Sarah.

EL SHADDAI

The *"Great Provider,"* God Almighty, El Shaddai, would provide a Redeemer who would come into this world to restore the lost sons of Adam's fallen race. This was what all of this was all about! This was the purpose and reason for the struggle! It was to look forward to the light that would ultimately dispel the darkness, the salvation that would ultimately dispel the sin, the life that would ultimately dispel the death, and the freedom that would ultimately dispel the bondage. All of this would be wrapped up in one Man, *"the Man Christ Jesus."*

Jacob again reiterated the glorious appearing of the Lord to him at Beth-el when the great promises were affirmed and reaffirmed.

A great multitude of people would come from Jacob, even as the patriarch reminded Joseph. In fact, about 200 years later, they would number approximately 2.5 to 3 million strong.

As well, Jacob reminded Joseph that Egypt was not their everlasting possession, but rather only a temporal possession. Canaan was that everlasting possession, and Canaan they would have. Joseph was to understand this and so were his two sons.

Let the reader understand that as it regards the land of Israel, even presently (2013), it belongs to Israel and not the Muslims or anyone else, and will belong to them forever and forever. When God said, *"everlasting possession,"* He meant exactly what He said.

OPPOSITION TO THE PROMISE

Though God promises something, it not at all means that Satan will not oppose the promise and actually the fulfillment of the promise. In fact, there is quite a distance between the promise and the possession. Satan will do everything within his power to keep the promise from being fulfilled. Let the reader understand that the one ingredient he will fight is faith, and it is because it is faith that will claim and possess the promise.

However, as faith possesses the promise, faith also dispels the opposition. Once again, allow me to state the fact that the faith of which I speak is always faith in *"Christ and Him crucified"* (I Cor. 1:23; 2:2). Even though Jacob would not have understood the terminology I have just used, still, this, as well, is what his faith would ultimately produce and, in fact, what it was meant to produce all along.

In essence, one might say that all in the Old Testament had faith in the prophetic Jesus, at least those who truly knew the Lord, while we now have faith in the historical Jesus, as well as the prophetic Jesus. Historically, He has come, lived, died, was resurrected, ascended, and is now exalted at the right hand of the Father on high (Heb. 1:2-3). Prophetically, He is coming again and is coming to rule and reign upon this earth for 1,000 years. During that time, Israel and every saint of God will reign with Him. To be sure, we speak of every saint who has ever lived, even from the dawn of time, whoever they may have been (I Thess. 4:13-18).

THE STRUGGLE OF FAITH

Let the believer always know and understand that the struggle in which he is engaged and, in fact, will be engaged until the trump sounds or the Lord calls us home is a struggle of faith. That's the reason the great apostle told Timothy: *"Fight the good fight of faith, lay hold on eternal life, whereunto you are also called, and have professed a good profession before many witnesses"* (I Tim. 6:12).

While it is a fight, at the same time, it is a good fight because it is a fight that we will win. This fight lays hold on eternal life and *"professes a good profession before many witnesses."* This means that we are fighting the same fight of faith that Jacob fought and, in fact, all others who have gone on before us and have been victorious in this conflict.

This means that in the final, it is not a struggle with finances, with physical well-being, with domestic situations, or with social implications, but rather that which is spiritual. It all comes down to the promises of God that are ensconced in His Word, which proclaims our victorious supremacy. It is all brought about because of who Jesus is and what Jesus did, and I speak of His finished work on the Cross. That is the fight of faith we are called upon to engage. It transcends all other struggles, and if we succeed in that, we succeed in all (Rom. 6:1-14; 8:1-11).

THE MESSAGE OF THE CROSS

The story of the Bible is the story of the Cross, even as the story of the Cross is the story of the Bible.

About 170 times in his 14 epistles, Paul used the term *"in Christ"* or one of its derivatives, such as *"in the Lord Jesus,"* *"in Him,"* etc. Those two words, *in Christ,* in effect, say it all.

It refers to Christ and what He did for us at the Cross, which He, in effect, did as our substitute and representative man (I Cor. 15:45-50). Simple faith in Christ places us in His death, burial, and resurrection (Rom. 6:3-5). The Cross is where the victory was won, and it is where the victory is maintained.

EPHRAIM AND MANASSEH

"And now your two sons, Ephraim and Manasseh, which were born unto you in the land of Egypt before I came unto you into Egypt are mine; as Reuben and Simeon, they shall be mine.

"And your issue, which you beget after them, shall be yours, and shall be called after the name of their brethren in their inheritance.

"And as for me, when I came from Padan, Rachel died by me in the land of Canaan in the way, when yet there was but a little way to come unto Ephrath: and I buried her there in the way of Ephrath; the same is Beth-lehem" (Gen. 48:5-7).

The Holy Spirit through Jacob would now claim the two sons of Joseph, in effect, as his own sons even though they were actually his grandsons. He claimed them on the same level as his first two sons, Reuben and Simeon. Concerning this, Horton said: *"By this Jacob indicated he was bypassing the older sons and was making sure that Joseph would get the double portion of the birthright. This would apply only to Ephraim and Manasseh. Any other children Joseph might have would get their inheritance through Ephraim and Manasseh. Jacob named Ephraim first in anticipation of the leadership Ephraim would have."*

THE DOUBLE CLAIM

Jacob first recited the gift of the land of Canaan to him by God (Gen. 48:3-4), then making Joseph his firstborn (Gen. 48:22), he adopted Joseph's two sons as his own, actually setting the younger above the elder.

In effect, Joseph had a double claim; he merited the birthright, and also, he was the firstborn of Rachel, who was Jacob's true wife.

By Jacob taking Ephraim and Manasseh, Joseph's sons, as his own, this filled out the complement of 13 sons. He had 11, and these two would make 13, as is obvious, which were needed to fill out the entirety of the Twelve Tribes of Israel plus the priestly tribe, totaling 13.

WHO ARE THESE?

"And Israel beheld Joseph's sons, and said, Who are these?

"And Joseph said unto his father, They are my sons, whom God has given me in this place. And he said, Bring them, I pray you, unto me, and I will bless them" (Gen. 48:8-9).

Pulpit Commentary says: *"That Jacob did not at first discern the presence of these two boys shows that his adoption of them into the number of the theocratic family was prompted not by accidental impulse of a natural affection excited through beholding these young men, but by the inward promptings of the Spirit of God."*

None of this that Jacob was doing was contrived out of his own mind. He was led by the Holy Spirit in every action. In fact, making these two sons of Joseph his own finished out the complement that God intended, as stated, of the 13 tribes of Israel. They would stay in Egypt some 215 years. At least, that's how long it was from the time that Jacob went into Egypt and when they would go out under Moses, delivered by the mighty power of God. They would go out approximately 3 million strong.

ISRAEL

As Joseph stood that day before his father, his two sons, Ephraim and Manasseh, were with him. The implication seems to be that Jacob could dimly see them but not well enough to make out who they were. If, in fact, my statements are correct, this shows that Jacob was not entirely blind but nearly so. At any rate, he did not recognize the two boys even though he had been speaking of them to Joseph.

In Verse 8, the Holy Spirit refers to Jacob as Israel because what he was doing was a work and word of faith.

The two sons of Joseph stood before the aged patriarch, and he blessed them. A further work of the Spirit took place.

THE EYES OF FAITH

"Now the eyes of Israel were dim for age, so that he could not see. And he brought them near unto him; and he kissed them, and embraced them.

"And Israel said unto Joseph, I had not thought to see your face: and, lo, God has shown me also your seed.

"And Joseph brought them out from between his knees, and he bowed himself with his face to the earth" (Gen. 48:10-12).

A number of things are said in these verses:

First of all, Jacob was referred to as Israel, once again signaling his great faith. In fact, the entirety of this chapter throbs with faith. Jacob was referred to as Israel nine times in this one chapter. It speaks of faith. It's not so much that Jacob's faith was perfect, for possibly, that cannot be said of anyone. However, he had carried out, and was carrying out, all that God had called him to do, and without reservation.

His eyes, naturally speaking, may have been dim because of age, but even though he could little see in the physical sense, concerning his faith, he had never had greater illumination. In effect, he could now see as he had never seen before.

He now recalled to Joseph that he had never thought to see Joseph again; however, not only had he seen Joseph, but he had also seen Joseph's sons, his grandsons. He gave God all the praise and glory for this, even as he should have done.

As Jacob said these things, Joseph bowed low before his father, realizing the tremendous import of what was being said.

THE BLESSING

"And Joseph took them both, Ephraim in his right hand toward Israel's left hand, and Manasseh in his left hand toward Israel's right hand, and brought them near unto him.

"And Israel stretched out his right hand, and laid it upon Ephraim's head, who was the younger, and his left hand upon Manasseh's head, guiding his hands wittingly; for Manasseh was the firstborn.

"And he blessed Joseph, and said, God, before whom my fathers Abraham and Isaac did walk, the God which fed me all my life long unto this day,

"The Angel which redeemed me from all evil, bless the lads; and let my name be named on them, and the name of my fathers Abraham and Isaac; and let them grow into a multitude in the midst of the earth" (Gen. 48:13-16).

The blessing that Jacob bestowed upon these two boys was no empty blessing, but rather rich with eternal wealth, even as faith very well knew.

Jacob feared the influence of Egypt upon his sons. His nature led him all his life to grasp at wealth and position, but now faith shined brightly, and he earnestly pointed Joseph and his sons to the true riches promised by God.

In fact, they actually were in great danger. Joseph was governor of all of Egypt, and brilliant prospects were within his reach for his children. The aged patriarch urged him not to make his home in Egypt but to set his heart in Canaan.

BY FAITH

Just before Jacob blessed these young men, the aged patriarch retook his staff and, leaning upon it so as not to fall, bowed in grateful worship before God. This was the time of which Paul spoke when he wrote: *"By faith Jacob, when he was a dying, blessed both the sons of Joseph; and worshipped, leaning upon the top of his staff"* (Heb. 11:21). Strengthening himself once more upon the bed, he bid his grandsons yet again to come near him, and crossing his hands, he blessed them. As stated, it was no empty blessing but was rich with eternal wealth, even as faith very well knew.

All of this shows that Jacob was not set upon the wealth of his luxurious bedchamber that Joseph, no doubt, had provided for him, but was far away in God's chosen land. If he for a moment did lie upon such a costly couch, yet was he a worshipper of God thereon.

THE PROMISE

Manasseh was the firstborn, and Joseph expected Jacob to give him the greater part of the blessing. However, the Holy Spirit, who alone knows all the future, told Jacob to put his right hand, which pronounced the greater blessing, upon the head of Ephraim, who was the younger.

He specified that the blessing about to be pronounced came from God, who had guided both Abraham and Isaac, and who had also guided him all the days of his life.

He gave the Lord the praise for redeeming him from all evil, and then said, *"Let my name be named on them, and the name of my fathers Abraham and Isaac."* Finally, he said, *"Let them grow into a multitude in the midst of the earth."*

The first pertained to the promise, and I speak of the God of Abraham, Isaac, and Jacob, while the second spoke of blessing. The promise had to do with the coming Redeemer, who definitely did come. The blessing concerning the multitude is yet to be fulfilled, but definitely will be fulfilled in the coming millennium when Israel will be the leading nation on the earth.

EPHRAIM

"And when Joseph saw that his father laid his right hand upon the head of Ephraim, it displeased him: and he held

up his father's hand, to remove it from Ephraim's head unto Manasseh's head.

"And Joseph said unto his father, Not so, my father: for this is the firstborn; put your right hand upon his head.

"And his father refused, and said, I know it, my son, I know it: he also shall become a people, and he also shall be great: but truly his younger brother shall be greater than he, and his seed shall become a multitude of nations.

"And he blessed them that day, saying, In you shall Israel bless, saying, God make you as Ephraim and as Manasseh: and he set Ephraim before Manasseh.

"And Israel said unto Joseph, Behold, I die: but God shall be with you, and bring you again unto the land of your fathers.

"Moreover I have given to you one portion above your brethren, which I took out of the hand of the Amorite with my sword and with my bow" (Gen. 48:17-22).

Joseph, thinking his father's dim eyesight had caused him to confuse the two boys, proceeded to take the right hand of the patriarch from the head of Ephraim and place it on the head of Manasseh, who was, in fact, the firstborn. However, Jacob refused to do this and, in effect, said that he knew what he was doing.

THE HOLY SPIRIT

Jacob had selected the younger first instead of the older simply because the Holy Spirit had guided him accordingly. Ephraim, although the younger, would be the greater of the two tribes and, in fact, would be greater than any of the Twelve Tribes of Israel, with the exception of Judah.

Jacob wanted Joseph and his two grandsons, as well as all of his sons, to know that even though they were greatly blessed in Egypt, Canaan was, in fact, their home. He bid them to always look to yonder land.

Jacob told Joseph that the land was a doubly precious land; first, because God gave it to him; and second, because there he buried Rachel. In effect, he said to Joseph, *"That land should be doubly precious to you because of these two facts."*

All of this presents a scene of touching tenderness! The aged eyes of the dying patriarch glowed once more with the love of early manhood. He looked eagerly into Joseph's eyes as much to say, *"Joseph, I loved her, and she was your mother."* Thus, he laid these two great pleas upon the heart of Joseph so that they should save him from making Egypt his country.

We aren't told exactly what Jacob meant by his statement, *"Which I took out of the hand of the Amorite with my sword and with my bow."* It could mean one of two things, or even both: this very well could have been a conflict with the Amorites of which we are given no information. As well, it could speak of the coming day when Israel would vanquish this foe, which is probably the meaning.

Jacob giving the blessing to the sons of Joseph, especially the double blessing to Ephraim, in essence, was giving it to Joseph. Esau sold his birthright, and Reuben forfeited his. Jacob, therefore, could bestow it on whom he would.

"We praise You, O God!
"For the Son of Your love,
"For Jesus who died,
"And is now gone above."

"We praise You, O God!
"For Your Spirit of light,
"Who has shown us our Saviour,
"And scattered our night."

"All glory and praise
"To the Lamb who was slain,
"Who has borne all our sins,
"And has cleansed every stain."

"Revive us again;
"Fill each heart with Your love,
"May each soul be rekindled
"With fire from above."

JOSEPH

CHAPTER

15

THE PROPHECY

CHAPTER FIFTEEN

THE PROPHECY

"Joseph is a fruitful bough, even a fruitful bough by a well; whose branches run over the wall:

"The archers have sorely grieved him, and shot at him, and hated him:

"But his bow abode in strength, and the arms of his hands were made strong by the hands of the mighty God of Jacob; (from thence is the shepherd, the stone of Israel:)

"Even by the God of your father, who shall help you; and by the Almighty, who shall bless you with blessings of heaven above, blessings of the deep that lie under, blessings of the breasts, and of the womb:

"The blessings of your father have prevailed above the blessings of my progenitors unto the utmost bound of the everlasting hills: they shall be on the head of Joseph, and on the crown of the head of him who was separate from his brethren" (Gen. 49:22-26).

At this time, Jacob blessed all of his sons, and at the same time, gave them a word concerning the future, which proved to be exact in detail. We have dealt only with Joseph because Joseph is the subject of this book.

A TYPE OF CHRIST

Joseph, as Judah, is a type of Christ, hence, the flowing and glowing superlatives.

Judah is portrayed as Christ in His sufferings, while Joseph is portrayed as Christ in His millennial blessings. It is the same as David portraying Christ in His conquering mode, while Solomon portrays Christ in His rulership of peace and prosperity.

Consequently, this of Joseph portrays Christ in the coming kingdom age.

He is described first of all as a *"fruitful bough,"* and greater still, *"a fruitful bough by a well."* In fact, the branches are so outspreading and so full of fruit that they *"run over the wall,"* which means that in that coming age, there will be an abundance of everything.

As Joseph's brethren hated him, likewise, Israel hated Christ and, in fact, crucified Him. However, what they didn't seem to know was the One they hated was actually *"the Shepherd, the Stone of Israel."* As such, God would raise Him from the dead, with His *"arms being made strong by the hands of the mighty God of Jacob."*

BLESSINGS

As Joseph is a type of Christ, the Holy Spirit through the patriarch is here actually referring to Christ. It is Christ alone who enjoys the blessings of the Father, and those blessings come upon Him in every manner. For instance, He has all blessings from Heaven, and, as well, the earth will literally spew out blessings upon Him. The *"blessings of the breasts, and of the womb,"* proclaim the fact that untold numbers will be born into the kingdom of God, all because of what Christ did at the Cross, and, in effect, will be His brothers and sisters.

As well, He has blessed more than the patriarchs, prophets, and apostles of old, and as long as the hills endure, His blessings will endure.

These blessings shall rest on the head of Christ and shall settle on His crown, for He is *King of kings and Lord of lords.*

BLESSINGS ON BELIEVERS

The believer must understand that our blessings are received only through Christ and what He did for us at the Cross. Apart from Christ, God blesses no one, for apart from Christ, God cannot bless anyone.

Jesus is our substitute and, in effect, our representative man (I Cor. 15:45-47). As the federal head of all believers, He stands in our place. In other words, God does not really look to us or at us, but rather to Him and at Him. Whatever He is, we are.

The way we obtain this is by faith. When we use that statement, we are referring to faith in Christ and what He did for us in His finished work on the Cross. Faith in Him exclusively guarantees to such a believer all that Christ is. If it is proper faith, it always refers to what He did on the Cross,

Every Christian wants blessings, and rightly so! However, we must understand that God does not bless us because of our works, labors, enthusiasm, zeal, or efforts on His behalf, as dedicated as all of these things might be. Our blessings come exclusively through Christ and are obtained strictly by faith.

Whenever our faith is properly placed, all that is said here regarding Joseph, i.e., Christ, applies to us as well. They are blessings of every description and from every direction.

Now, what I've told you in these previous few paragraphs constitutes a great truth. As we've already stated, every believer wants blessings, but there's only one way those blessings can be obtained.

Because it's so important, let us say it again: God does not really bless individuals per se, whomever they might be; at least, one might say that He doesn't bless us apart from Christ. The blessings rest upon Christ, and rest upon Christ exclusively. When we have faith in Him, which refers to what He did at the Cross, then His blessings become our blessings.

BLESSINGS NOW

Since the Lord spoke to my heart sometime back concerning blessings, I have watched the blessings become more and more pronounced.

I personally feel that the Lord is going to give us more souls, more people delivered, more lives changed, more believers baptized with the Holy Spirit, and more people truly healed by the power of God than we have ever previously known. In fact, we are in the preparation stages of that at this moment (2013).

I believe the Lord wants this Message of the Cross to be spread over the entirety of the earth. As well, I believe it is what the Holy Spirit is presently saying to the churches, *"Jesus Christ and Him crucified."*

That's why Paul said: *"For Christ sent me not to baptize, but to preach the Gospel: not with wisdom of words, lest the Cross of Christ should be made of none effect.*

"For the preaching of the Cross is to them who perish foolishness; but unto us who are saved it is the power of God" (I Cor. 1:17-18).

> *"My soul today is thirsting for living streams divine,*
> *"To sweep from highest heaven to this poor heart*
>   *of mine;*
> *"I stand upon the promise, in Jesus' name I plead*
> *"O send the gracious current to satisfy my need."*

"I see the clouds arising, the mercy clouds of love,
"That come to bring refreshing down from the
throne above,
"The earnest of the shower, just now to us is given,
"And now we wait, expecting the floods of grace
from Heaven."

"The showers of grace are falling, the tide is rolling in,
"The floodtide of salvation, with power to cleanse
from sin;
"It's surging through my being, and takes my sin away,
"It keeps me shouting glory! Through all the happy day."

"It's coming, yes it's coming, it's coming down this hour,
"A torrent of salvation in saving, cleansing power,
"Hear the billows surging, I see them mount and roll;
"O glory, hallelujah! They're sweeping through
my soul."

JOSEPH

16

THE DEATH OF JACOB

CHAPTER SIXTEEN

THE DEATH OF JACOB

"And when Jacob had made an end of commanding his sons, he gathered up his feet into the bed, and yielded up the ghost, and was gathered unto his people.

"And Joseph commanded his servants the physicians to embalm his father: and the physicians embalmed Israel.

"And forty days were fulfilled for him; for so are fulfilled the days of those which are embalmed: and the Egyptians mourned for him 70 days" (Gen. 49:33; 50:2-3).

The last hours of the great patriarch Jacob were filled with prophecies and predictions concerning the Twelve Tribes of Israel, which would ultimately bring the Redeemer into the world. Actually, because this book is about Joseph, we only dealt with that part of the great prophecies.

Jacob died when the prophecy was completed, but he did not die until it was completed.

The great patriarch had ultimately realized that which God had called him to do. The main thing is, he had kept the faith that was once delivered unto Abraham and his father Isaac. He had not allowed that torch to fall to the ground or even be dimmed. At his death, it burned brightly and, in fact, brighter than ever.

The embalmers were not normally physicians. So, it is more than likely that Joseph commanded the physicians to superintend the process, which they, no doubt, did.

According to Pliny, the study of medicine originated in Egypt. The physicians employed by Joseph were those attached to his own household or the court practitioners, which the latter was probably the case.

Due to the fact that they were going to have to take Jacob's body the long distance back to Canaan, which would take several weeks, Jacob would have had to have the most extensive process.

PHARAOH

"And when the days of his mourning were past, Joseph spoke unto the house of Pharaoh, saying, If now I have found grace in your eyes, speak, I pray you, in the ears of Pharaoh, saying,

"My father made me swear, saying, Lo, I die: in my grave which I have dug for me in the land of Canaan, there shall you bury me. Now therefore let me go up, I pray you, and bury my father, and I will come again.

"And Pharaoh said, Go up, and bury your father, according as he made you swear" (Gen. 50:4-6).

The grandeur of Jacob's funeral procession must have been a wonder to behold. It is amazing to think of this great patriarch, a pilgrim all his life, being carried to his final resting place by the grandeur of mighty Egypt. It is one of the few times in history that the world recognized the greatness that was among them.

Abraham and Isaac, both very wealthy men, were buried in the tomb of Machpelah. There Jacob was laid to rest, as well, with all the glory and riches of Egypt; however, none of them took anything with them *but their faith.*

Joseph, in making his request to Pharaoh, did not go in directly to that monarch, but rather spoke to him through the members of the royal household.

According to Egyptian custom, Joseph would have let his beard and hair grow during the time of mourning, which this appearance forbade him approaching the throne. Pharaoh's answer would, of course, be conveyed through the courtiers.

A VERY GREAT COMPANY

"And Joseph went up to bury his father: and with him went up all the servants of Pharaoh, the elders of his house, and all the elders of the land of Egypt,

"And all the house of Joseph, and his brethren, and his father's house: only their little ones, and their flocks, and their herds, they left in the land of Goshen.

"And there went up with him both chariots and horsemen: and it was a very great company.

"And they came to the threshingfloor of Atad, which is beyond Jordan, and there they mourned with a great and very sore lamentation: and he made a mourning for his father seven days.

"And when the inhabitants of the land, the Canaanites, saw the mourning in the floor of Atad, they said, This is a grievous mourning to the Egyptians: wherefore the name of it was called Abel-mizraim, which is beyond Jordan.

"And his sons did unto him according as he commanded them:

"For his sons carried him into the land of Canaan, and buried him in the cave of the field of Machpelah, which Abraham bought with the field for a possession of a buryingplace of Ephron the Hittite, before Mamre" (Gen. 50:7-13).

THE FUNERAL PROCESSION

This funeral procession must have been one of the largest ever conducted in Egypt up to that time. Of course, all the family of Jacob was present, with the exception of the babies and little children. As well, the household of Pharaoh and also the members of his cabinet attended, all accompanied by chariots and horsemen.

Funeral processions in Egypt were generally headed up by servants who led the way. They would be carrying tables laden with fruit, cakes, flowers, vases of ointment, wine, and other liquids, with three young geese and a calf for sacrifice, chairs and wooden tablets, napkins, and other things.

Then others followed bearing daggers, bows, fans, and the mummy cases in which the deceased and his ancestors had been kept previous to burial.

Next came a table of offerings, couches, boxes, and a chariot. After these things, men appeared with gold vases and more offerings. After these came the bearers of a sacred boat and the mysterious eyes of Osiris as the god of stability.

THE CAVE OF THE FIELD OF MACHPELAH

Placed on the consecrated boat, the hearse containing the mummy of the deceased was drawn by four oxen and by seven men under the direction of a superintendent who regulated the march of the funeral. Behind the hearse followed the male relations and friends of the deceased. They either beat their breasts or gave token of their sorrow by their silence and solemn steps as they walked, leaning on their long sticks. With these, the procession closed.

Of course, the procession described was only for a short distance. Consequently, while certainly having some of these trappings, of necessity, the funeral procession of Jacob would have been scaled down due to the long trip to Canaan.

Joseph had the entire procession to stop when they came to the *"threshingfloor of Atad,"* where they underwent a second mourning of seven days. Then Jacob was taken to the *"cave of the field of Machpelah,"* where Abraham and Isaac were buried. Sarah was also buried there along with Rebekah and Leah.

RESURRECTION

While the inhabitants of the land of Canaan did not know or understand the significance of these burials, the patriarchs readily understood what they were doing. God had promised them this land, and by faith, their burial in the land staked a claim not merely to the burying place, but to the entirety of this country that would one day be called Israel.

As well, there was something else in mind that did transcend all other principles, and I speak of resurrection. Even though the subject was then dim, still, their faith was sure as it regarded this miracle of miracles, which they believed that one day would happen. It has not yet happened, but we are 4,000 years closer than Abraham was when he was buried.

In fact, the Resurrection, i.e., *"the Rapture,"* could take place at any moment.

Concerning that coming event, the great Apostle Paul said: *"But I would not have you to be ignorant, brethren, concerning them which are asleep, that you sorrow not, even as others which have no hope.*

"For if we believe that Jesus died and rose again, even so them also which sleep in Jesus will God bring with Him.

"For this we say unto you by the Word of the Lord, that we which are alive and remain unto the coming of the Lord shall not prevent them which are asleep.

"For the Lord Himself shall descend from Heaven with a shout, with the voice of the archangel, and with the trump of God: and the dead in Christ shall rise first:

"Then we which are alive and remain shall be caught up together with them in the clouds, to meet the Lord in the air: and so shall we ever be with the Lord.

"Wherefore comfort one another with these words" (I Thess. 4:13-18).

JOB

We do know that the Resurrection was known as early as Job, who was the son of Issachar, who was the son of Jacob. In other words, Job was the grandson of Jacob.

As well, the book of Job is probably the first book written as it regards the Bible, and was probably written by Moses in collaboration with Job, who was contemporary with Moses for some years.

Job said, *"If a man die, shall he live again? all the days of my appointed time will I wait, till my change come"* (Job 14:14).

Job would have learned of the Resurrection from his grandfather Jacob, who learned it from Isaac, who learned it from Abraham. No doubt, the doctrine was known from the very beginning.

Enoch, who lived about 1,200 years before Jacob, said, *"Behold, the Lord comes with ten thousands of His saints"* (Jude, Vs. 14).

This speaks of resurrection!

"Search me, O God, and know my heart today;
"Try me O Saviour, know my thoughts, I pray;
"See if there be some wicked way in me;
"Cleanse me from every sin, and set me free."

"I praise You Lord, for cleansing me from sin:
"Fulfill Your Word and make me pure within;
"Fill me with fire, where once I burned with shame;
"Grant my desire to magnify Your name."

"Lord, take my life, and make it wholly Thine:
"Fill my poor heart with Your great love Divine;
"Take all my will, my passion, self and pride;
"I now surrender: Lord, in me abide."

"O Holy Spirit, revival comes from Thee:
"Send a revival, start the work in me:
"Your Word declares You will supply our need:
"For blessing now, O Lord, I humbly plead."

JOSEPH

CHAPTER

17

THE LAST DAYS OF JOSEPH

CHAPTER SEVENTEEN

THE LAST DAYS OF JOSEPH

"And Joseph returned into Egypt, he, and his brothers, and all who went up with him to bury his father, after he had buried his father.

"And when Joseph's brothers saw that their father was dead, they said, Joseph will peradventure hate us, and will certainly requite us all the evil which we did unto him.

"And they sent a messenger unto Joseph, saying, Your father did command before he died, saying,

"So shall you say unto Joseph, Forgive, I pray you now, the trespass of your brothers, and their sin; for they did unto you evil: and now, we pray you, forgive the trespass of the servants of the God of your father. And Joseph wept when they spoke unto him" (Gen. 50:14-17).

Concerning this time, George Williams said: *"The incurable unbelief of the human heart is illustrated by the cruel thoughts of Joseph's brothers as to his affection for them. This unbelief moved Joseph to tears; and in his action and language he once more stands forth as, perhaps the most remarkable type of Christ in the entirety of the Bible."*

Joseph's brothers never did quite understand who their brother was or what he was. Now that Jacob was dead, they expected evil of Joseph. They did not, and even perhaps could not, understand that Joseph, being a type of Christ, would deal with them not with judgment but with mercy and grace. How beautiful it would be if the church, as well, could learn this simple and yet beautiful act of Joseph.

THE TRUTH

Upon arriving back in Egypt, the brothers sent a message to Joseph as it regarded the great sin they had committed against him those many years before. They claimed that Jacob had said before he died that they should ask Joseph to forgive them of this sin.

Many Jewish expositors consider that this was untrue, and that Jacob was never made aware of the fact that his sons had sold Joseph into slavery; however, there is too much evidence to the contrary.

It is almost impossible for the brothers to have told their father about Joseph being alive and the viceroy of Egypt without further relating their culpability in Joseph's disappearance. It was almost imperative that they confess to their father at that time.

They knew that very soon Jacob would see Joseph, and in their minds, they believed that Joseph would relate the truth to Jacob, whether, in fact, he would have or not. Once again, in their thinking, it would be much better for this terrible truth to first come from them, which it, no doubt, did.

Then again, it is highly unlikely that they would have lied to Joseph at this stage, claiming that Jacob had said such a thing when, in reality, he hadn't.

The terminology sounds like Jacob because the patriarch knew that the brothers were very concerned about this. So, he probably told them what to do, thereby, at least after a fashion, setting their minds at ease.

The messenger went before Joseph, with Joseph then sending for his brothers.

As he discussed with them what had happened so long before, he began to weep. The answer he would give them is most beautiful to behold and, as stated, is one of the most Christlike statements ever made by a human being.

GOD MEANT IT FOR GOOD

"And his brothers also went and fell down before his face; and they said, Behold, we be your servants.

"And Joseph said unto them, Fear not: for am I in the place of God?

"But as for you, you thought evil against me; but God meant it unto good, to bring to pass, as it is this day, to save much people alive.

"Now therefore do not fear: I will nourish you, and your little ones. And he comforted them, and spoke kindly unto them.

"And Joseph dwelt in Egypt, he, and his father's house: and Joseph lived an hundred and ten years" (Gen. 50:18-22).

As the brothers bowed down before him, by now knowing that all was forgiven, Joseph most probably asked them to stand as he spoke to them.

FEAR NOT

His question, *"Fear not: for am I in the place of God?"* in effect, says, *"I'm not the judge and, therefore, I do not punish. If any punishment is meted out, it will be God who does it and not me. You have nothing to fear from me."*

He then made a statement to them that proclaims to us a great truth.

Literally, he said to them, *"And you were thinking or meditating evil against me; Elohim was thinking or mediating for good."*

This tells us that God can take the evil practiced against us and can turn it around to our good, which He alone can do.

In effect, Joseph was saying that God had long before taken total charge of the affair, and everything was in His hands. As a result, he dared not insert his own will into the mix, but rather should trust the Lord implicitly. In effect, he was telling the brothers to do the same.

It was not God who caused Joseph's brothers to commit their foul deed against him, but He did permit it. As well, grace turned the terrible ugliness to glorious beauty. However, He can do this and, in fact, will do this only if we put everything in His hands. The moment we try to defend ourselves, thereby, seeking vengeance, we have taken it out of His hands, and the results will never be pleasant.

Joseph didn't talk down to his brothers. He told them that they must not fear. Furthermore, he promised to continue to see after them just as he had before their father Jacob had died. They were very fearful that once Jacob was dead, Joseph would use his great power to turn on them. In fact, he did use his great power, but it was to bless them and comfort them.

Out of all of this, one of the most beautiful statements is, *"And Joseph spoke kindly unto them."*

Verse 18 records the last of five times the brothers fulfilled the dreams of Joseph (Gen. 37:5-11). One day, in its greater fulfillment, which will be in the latter days, Israel will fall down at the feet of the Lord Jesus Christ, of whom Joseph was a type.

GREAT-GREAT GRANDCHILDREN

"And Joseph saw Ephraim's children of the third generation; the children also of Machir the son of Manasseh were brought up upon Joseph's knees" (Gen. 50:23).

Joseph lived to be 110 years of age and saw not only Ephraim's children but, as well, his children's children, which were Joseph's great-great-grandchildren.

These passages denote a happy time as Joseph grew older. He was the greatest blessing that Egypt ever knew. During the time that he held sway in that ancient land, little did Pharaoh know and understand what, in fact, was actually developing in his country.

Even though Egypt never really knew the Lord, and today, she is steeped in Islam with all of its attendant misery, in the coming kingdom age, Egypt will know the Lord Jesus Christ and will accept Him as Lord and Saviour.

The great Prophet Isaiah said: *"In that day shall there be an altar to the LORD in the midst of the land of Egypt, and a pillar at the border thereof to the LORD.*

"And it shall be for a sign and for a witness unto the LORD of Hosts in the land of Egypt: for they shall cry unto the LORD because of the oppressors, and He shall send them a Saviour, and a great One, and He shall deliver them.

"And the LORD shall be known to Egypt, and the Egyptians shall know the LORD in that day, and shall do sacrifice and oblation: yes, they shall vow a vow unto the LORD, and perform it" (Isa. 19:19-21).

Joseph was 110 years old when he died. He lived in Egypt 93 years, and his father's descendants lived there 215 years. This man who was sold as a slave into Egypt became a viceroy of the most powerful and richest nation on the face of the earth. He was without a doubt one of the most beautiful types of Christ who ever lived.

THE PROMISE

"And Joseph said unto his brothers, I die: and God will surely visit you, and bring you out of this land unto

the land which He swore to Abraham, to Isaac, and to Jacob" (Gen. 50:24).

As stated, Joseph was 110 years old, and he knew that he was about to die. He called his brethren around him, which, in effect, were his relatives. How many of his brothers were yet alive, we aren't told. The word *brothers* or *brethren* in the Hebrew can refer to actual brothers as we know such, their sons, or even sons' sons.

He told them that God would surely visit them and would bring them out of this land. He didn't say when, but the promise was given and, in a sense, was prophetic exactly as had been the prophecies of his father Jacob.

By his use of the names Abraham, Isaac, and Jacob, it portrays the fact that he was well acquainted with all the promises made to the patriarchs.

Also, in a sense, he considered himself, and rightly so, to have had a great part to play in all of this. In fact, he would be the last luminary until Moses, who would be born about 60 years later.

THE OATH

"And Joseph took an oath of the children of Israel, saying, God will surely visit you, and you shall carry up my bones from hence" (Gen. 50:25).

Joseph heard and believed what God had said to Abraham, to Isaac, and to Jacob as to the gift of Canaan, which would most surely come to pass.

Whenever the children of Israel left out of Egypt some 3 million strong, Moses was careful to take the bones of Joseph with him (Ex. 13:19).

It was some 40 years before the children of Israel would finally arrive in Canaan's fair land. By this time, Moses was gone, but Joshua would be very careful to bury the bones of Joseph in Shechem *"in a parcel of ground which Jacob bought of the sons of Hamor the father of Shechem for an hundred pieces of silver: and it became the inheritance of the children of Joseph"* (Josh. 24:32).

So, some 200 plus years after he died in Egypt, Joseph would finally come home to the place where he had been sold as a slave into Egypt. Joshua, no doubt, attended the burial.

JOSEPH

"So Joseph died, being an hundred and ten years old: and they embalmed him, and he was put in a coffin in Egypt" (Gen. 50:26).

Hebrews 11:22 draws attention to the double testimony of Joseph's faith when dying: God would surely redeem the children of Israel out of Egypt.

Likewise, Joshua, who attended Joseph's burial, was also 110 years old when he died.

Ellicott's Commentary said: *"With the death of Joseph ends the preparation for the formation of a chosen race. Summoned from a remote city upon the Persian Gulf to Canaan, Abraham had wandered there as a stranger, and*

Isaac and Jacob had followed in his steps. But in Canaan the race could never have multiplied largely; for there were races already there too powerful to permit of this rapid increase.

"Abraham and Lot, Esau and Jacob, had been compelled to separate; but now, under Joseph, they had been placed in a large, fertile, and well-nigh uninhabited region. The few who dwelt there were, as far as we can judge, of the Semitic stock, and whatsoever immigrants came from time to time were also of the same race, and we speak of Shem, and were soon enrolled in the clan of some Hebrew chief. And thus all was ready for their growth into a nation; and when we next read of them they had multiplied into a people so vast that Egypt was afraid of them."

Joseph finished this course with joy, even as did Jacob his father, and so can we if our faith is totally and completely in Christ, to whom the patriarchs ever pointed.

> "There shall be showers of blessing:
> "This is the promise of love;
> "There shall be seasons refreshing,
> "Sent from the Saviour above."

> "There shall be showers of blessing:
> "Precious reviving again;
> "Over the hills and the valleys,
> "Sound of abundance of rain."

"There shall be showers of blessing:
"Send them upon us, O Lord;
"Grant to us now a refreshing,
"Come, now honor Your Word."

"There shall be showers of blessing:
"Oh, that today they might fall,
"Now as to God we're confessing,
"Now as on Jesus we call!"

BIBLIOGRAPHY

CHAPTER 1

Stanley M. Horton, *Genesis: The Promise of Blessing*, World Library Press, Missouri, 1996, pg. 132.

H.D.M. Spence, *The Pulpit Commentary: Genesis*, Grand Rapids, Eerdmans Publishing Company, 1978.

Ibid.

C.H. Mackintosh, *Notes on the Book of Genesis*, Loizeaux Brothers, New York, 1880, pg. 316.

CHAPTER 4

Matthew Henry & Thomas Scott, *A Commentary upon the Holy Bible: Genesis to Deuteronomy*, The Religious Tract Society, 1836, pg. 98.

CHAPTER 6

Stanley M. Horton, *Genesis: The Promise of Blessing*, World Library Press, Missouri, 1996 pg 165.

CHAPTER 11

H.D.M. Spence, *The Pulpit Commentary: Genesis*, Grand Rapids, Eerdmans Publishing Company, 1978.

H.D.M. Spence, *The Pulpit Commentary: Genesis 45:14-15*, Grand Rapids, Eerdmans Publishing Company, 1978.

CHAPTER 13

Stanley M. Horton, *Genesis: The Promise of Blessing*, World Library Press, Missouri, 1996, pg. 187.

C.H. Mackintosh, *Notes on the Book of Genesis*, Loizeaux Brothers, New York, 1880, pg. 332.

CHAPTER 14

Stanley M. Horton, *Genesis: The Promise of Blessing*, World Library Press, Missouri, 1996, pg. 188.

H.D.M. Spence, *The Pulpit Commentary: Genesis*, Grand Rapids, Eerdmans Publishing Company, 1978.

CHAPTER 17

George Williams, *William's Complete Bible Commentary*, Grand Rapids, Kregel Publications, 1994, pg. 43.

Ellicott's Commentary on the Whole Bible, Zondervan Publishing House, Grand Rapids, 1970, pg. 175.

ABOUT EVANGELIST JIMMY SWAGGART

The Rev. Jimmy Swaggart is a Pentecostal evangelist whose anointed preaching and teaching has drawn multitudes to the Cross of Christ since 1956.

As an author, he has written more than 50 books, commentaries, study guides, and The Expositor's Study Bible, which has sold more than 1.5 million copies.

As an award-winning musician and singer, Brother Swaggart has recorded more than 50 Gospel albums and sold nearly 16 million recordings worldwide.

For nearly six decades, Brother Swaggart has channeled his preaching and music ministry through multiple media venues including print, radio, television and the Internet.

In 2010, Jimmy Swaggart Ministries launched its own cable channel, SonLife Broadcasting Network, which airs 24 hours a day to a potential viewing audience of more than 1 billion people around the globe.

Brother Swaggart also pastors Family Worship Center in Baton Rouge, Louisiana, the church home and headquarters of Jimmy Swaggart Ministries.

Jimmy Swaggart Ministries materials can be found at **www.jsm.org**.

NOTES

NOTES